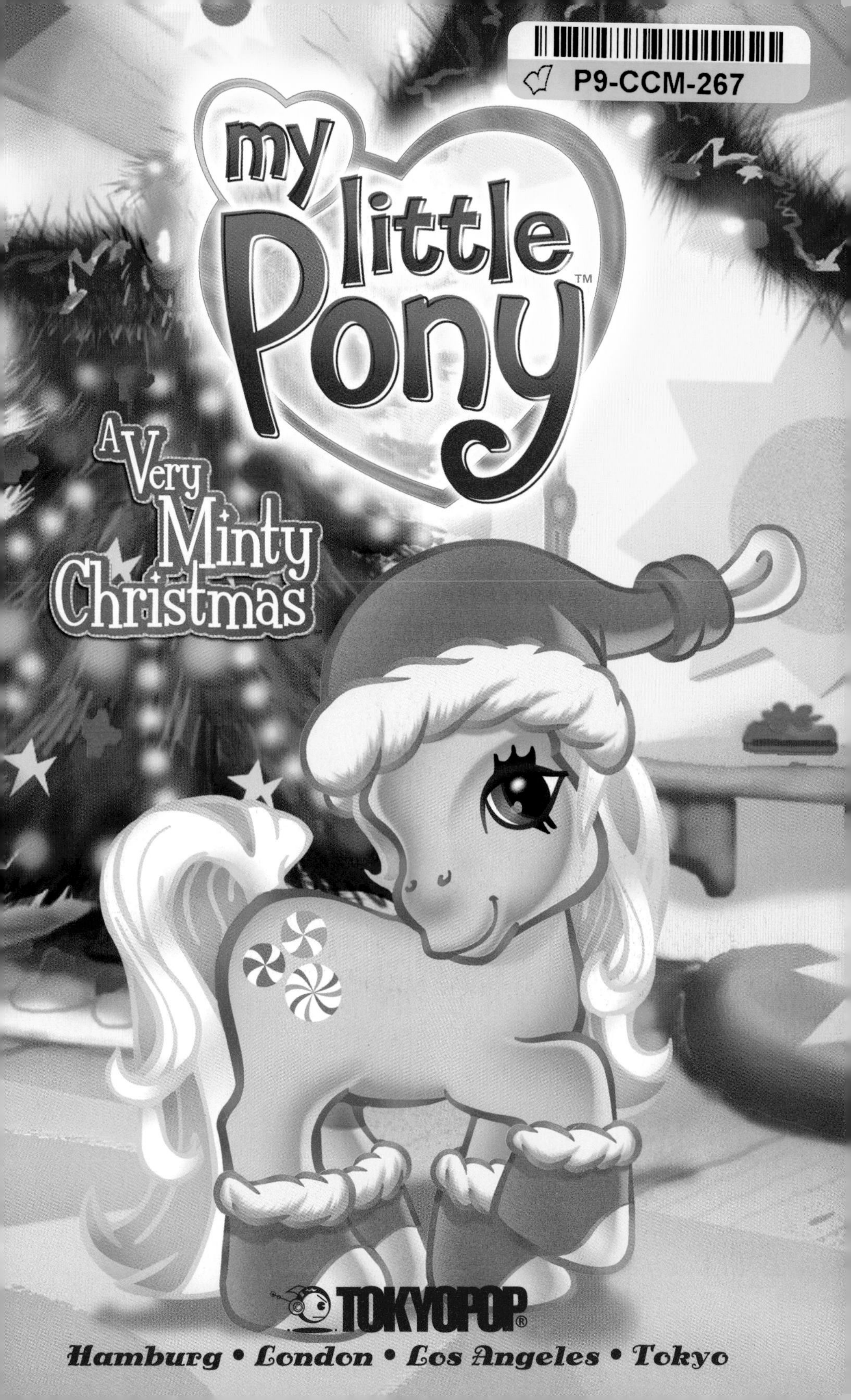
my little Pony™
A Very Minty Christmas
TOKYOPOP®
Hamburg • London • Los Angeles • Tokyo

Editor - Erin Stein
Graphic Designer and Letterer - Peter Sattler
Cover Designer - Seth Cable
Graphic Artist - Anna Kernbaum

Production Managers - Jennifer Miller and Mutsumi Miyazaki
Senior Designer - Anna Kernbaum
Senior Editor - Elizabeth Hurchalla
Managing Editor - Jill Freshney
VP of Production - Ron Klamert
Publisher & Editor in Chief - Mike Kiley
President & C.O.O. - John Parker
C.E.O. - Stuart Levy

E-mail: info@tokyopop.com
Come visit us online at www.TOKYOPOP.com

A ⊙TOKYOPOP® Cine-Manga® Book
TOKYOPOP Inc.
5900 Wilshire Blvd., Suite 2000
Los Angeles, CA 90036

My Little Pony Volume 2: A Very Minty Christmas

ISBN: 1-59816-001-X

First TOKYOPOP® printing: October 2005

10 9 8 7 6 5 4 3 2 1

Printed in the USA

my little pony™

A Very Minty Christmas™

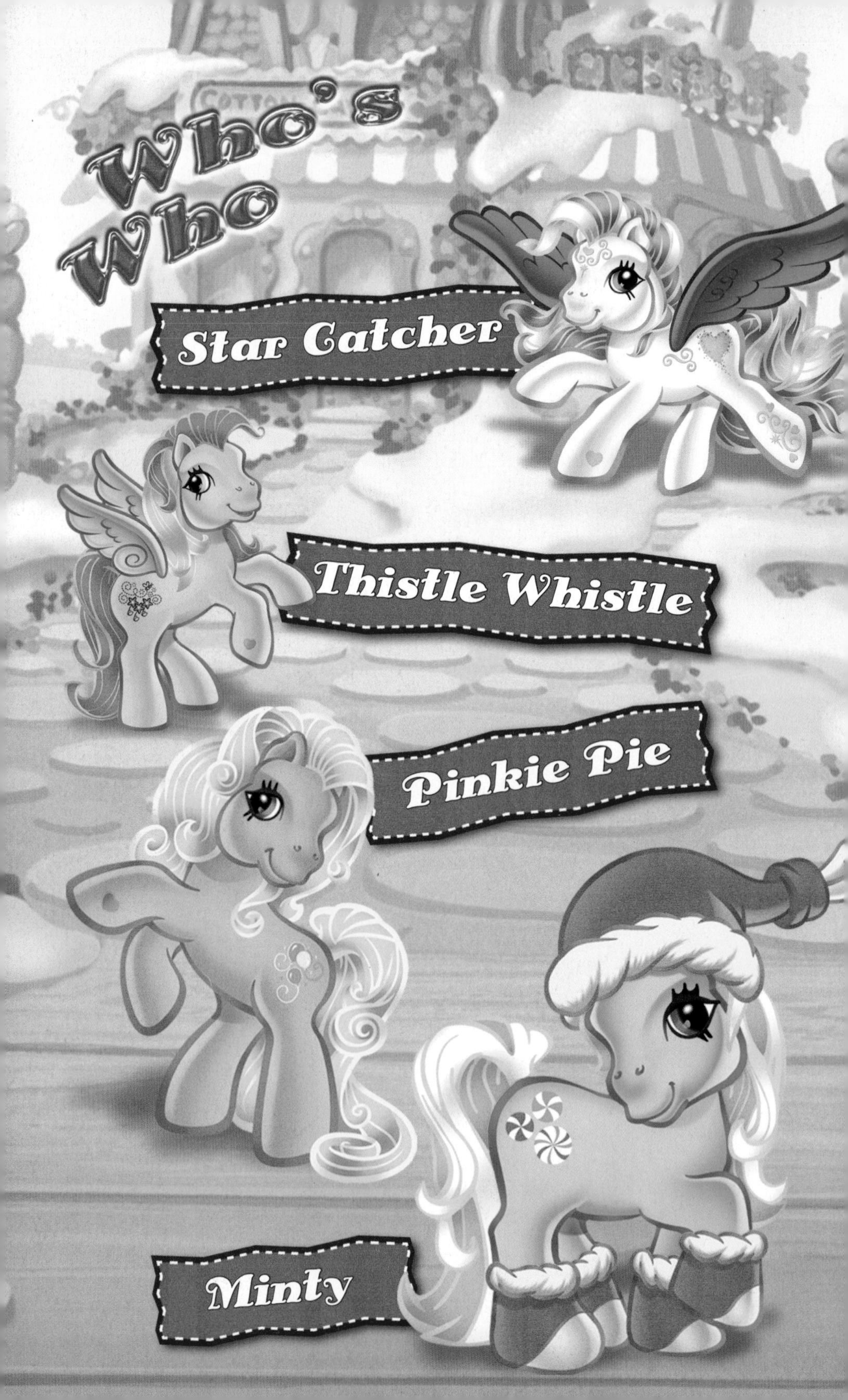

Who's Who
Star Catcher
Thistle Whistle
Pinkie Pie
Minty

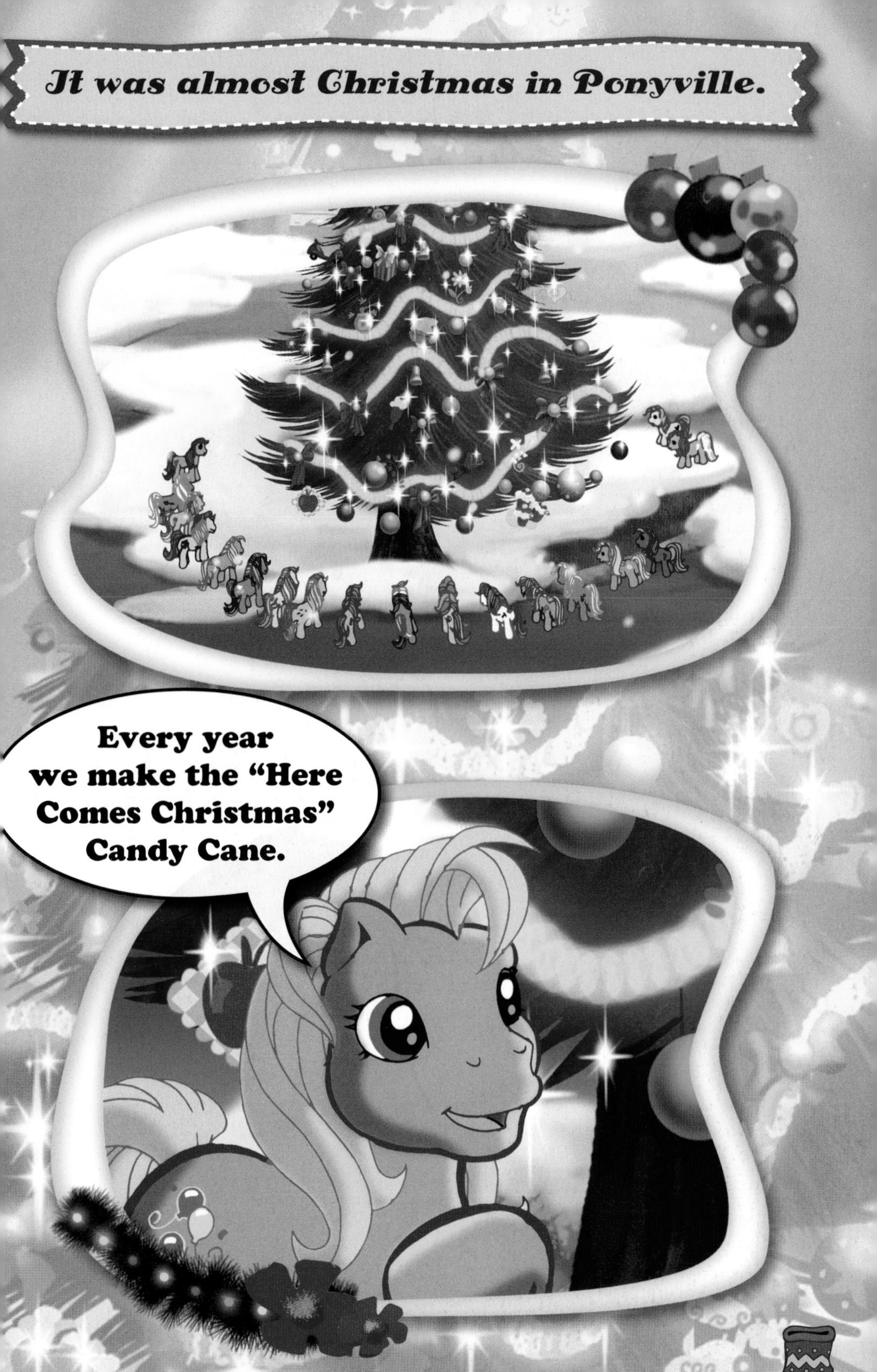
It was almost Christmas in Ponyville.
Every year we make the "Here Comes Christmas" Candy Cane.

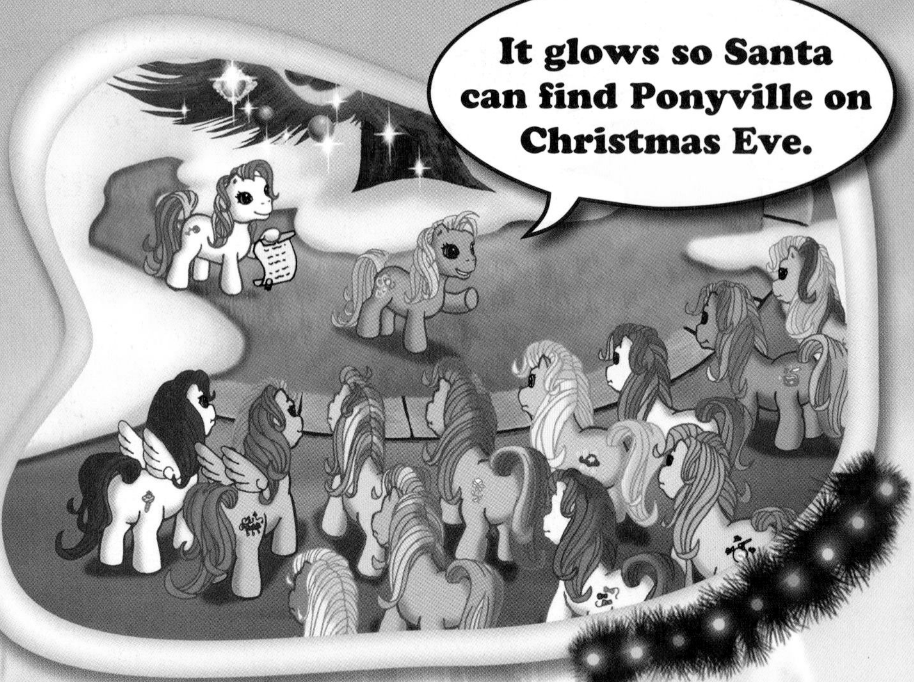
It glows so Santa can find Ponyville on Christmas Eve.

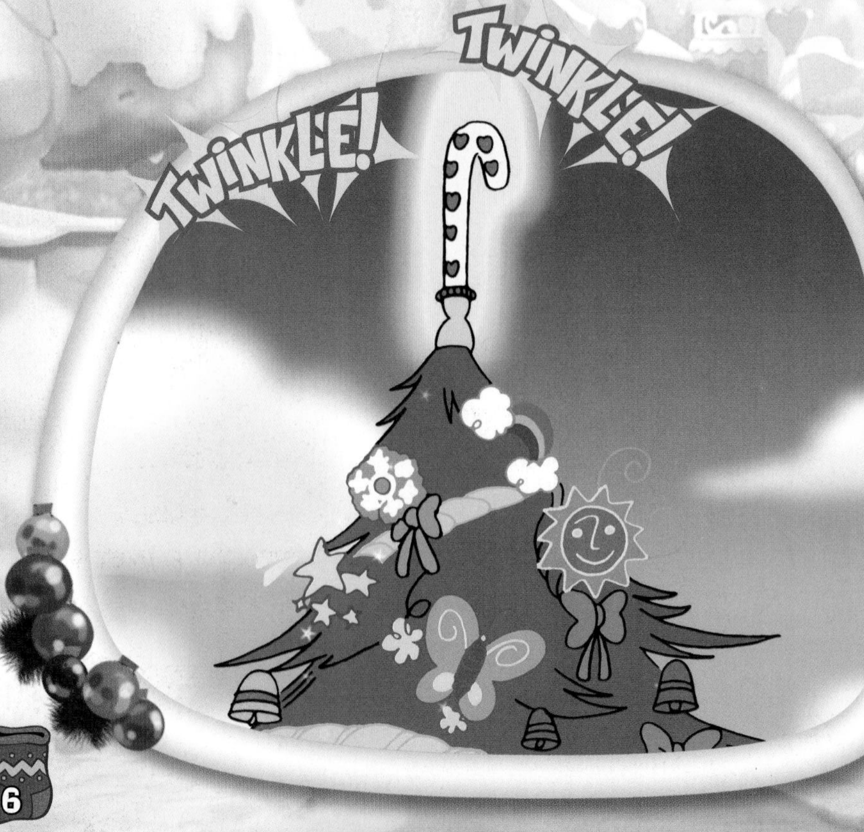
TWINKLE!
TWINKLE!

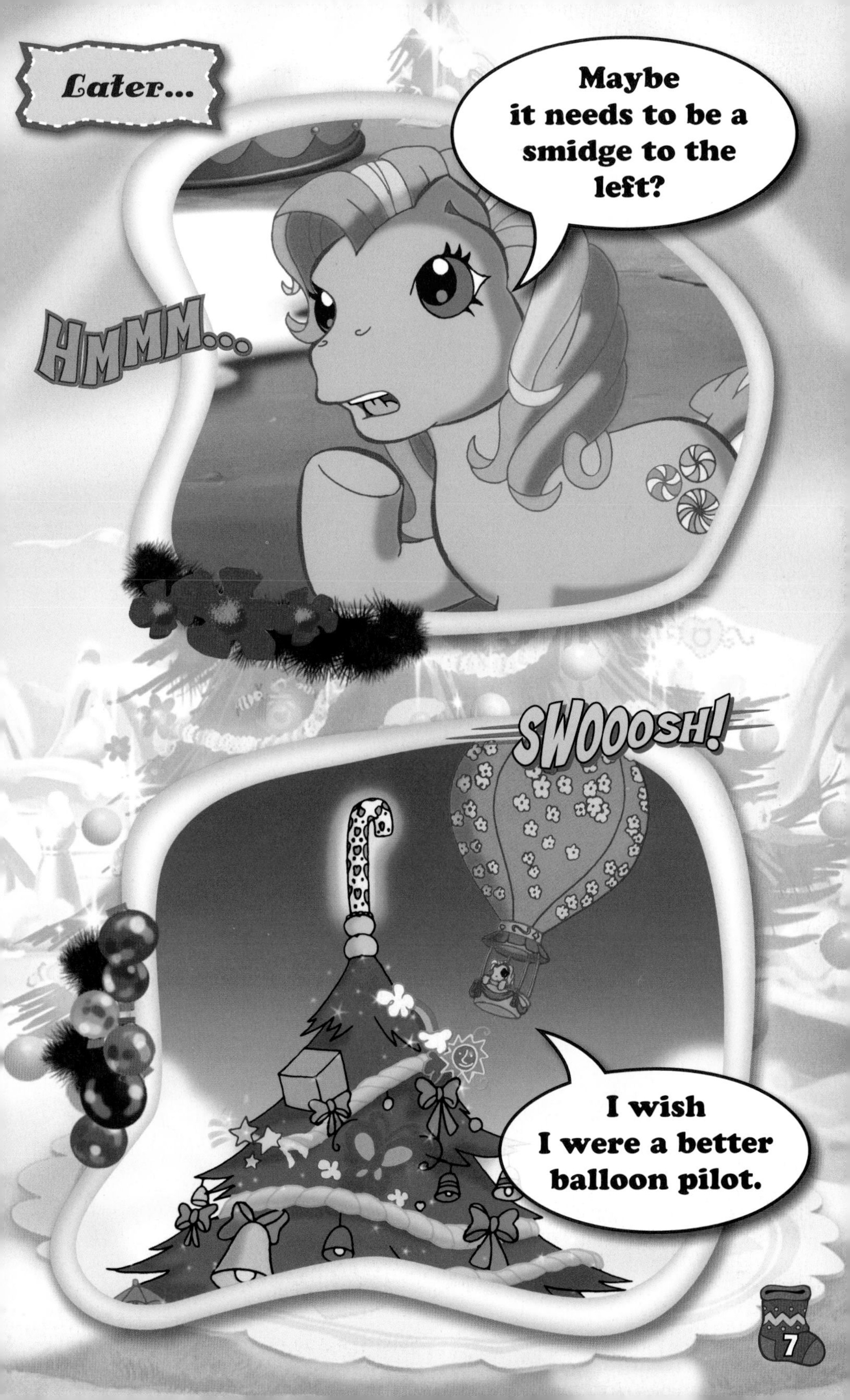
Later...
Maybe it needs to be a smidge to the left?
HMMM...
SWOOOSH!
I wish I were a better balloon pilot.

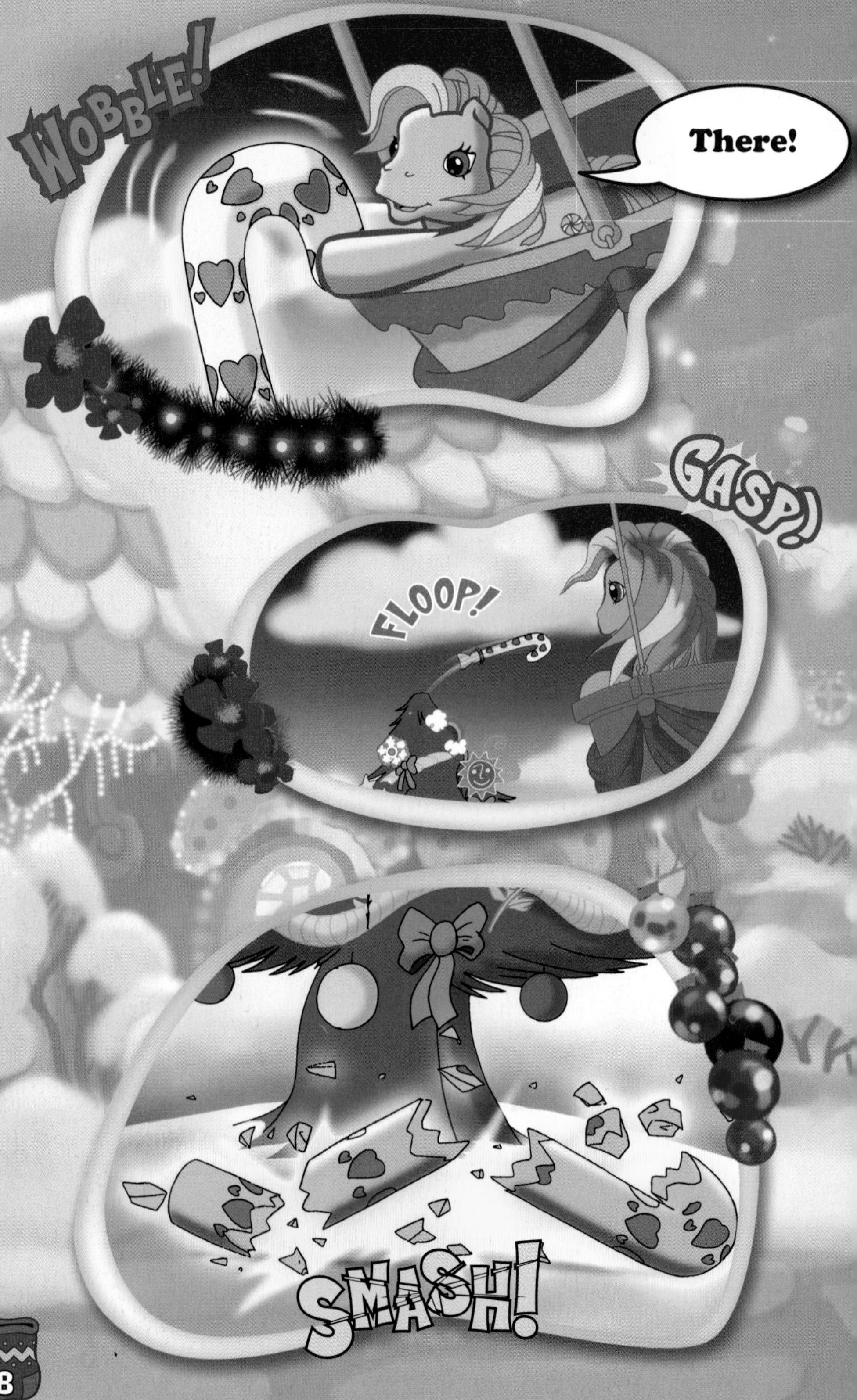
WOBBLE!
There!
GASP!
FLOOP!
SMASH!

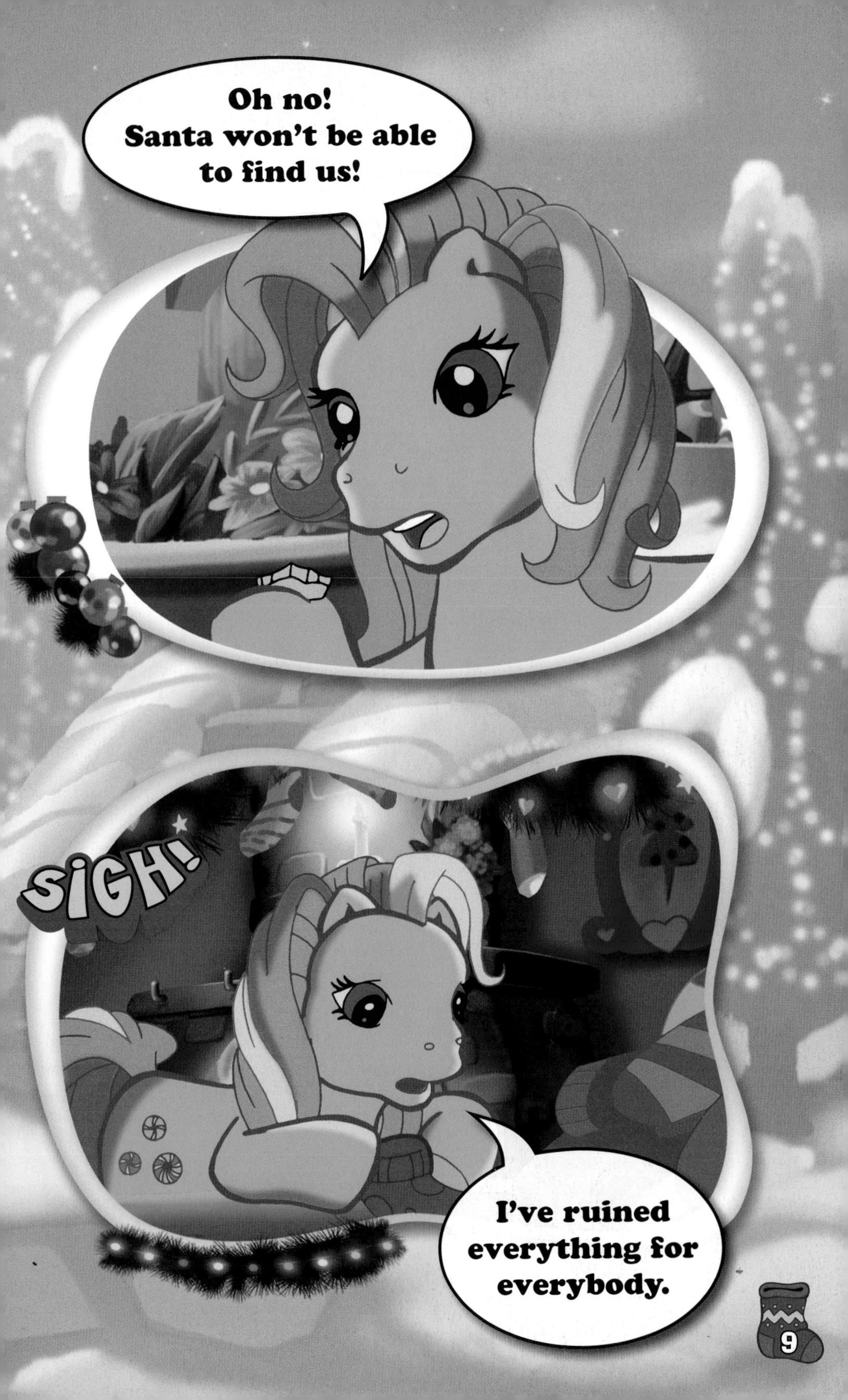
Oh no! Santa won't be able to find us!
SIGH!
I've ruined everything for everybody.

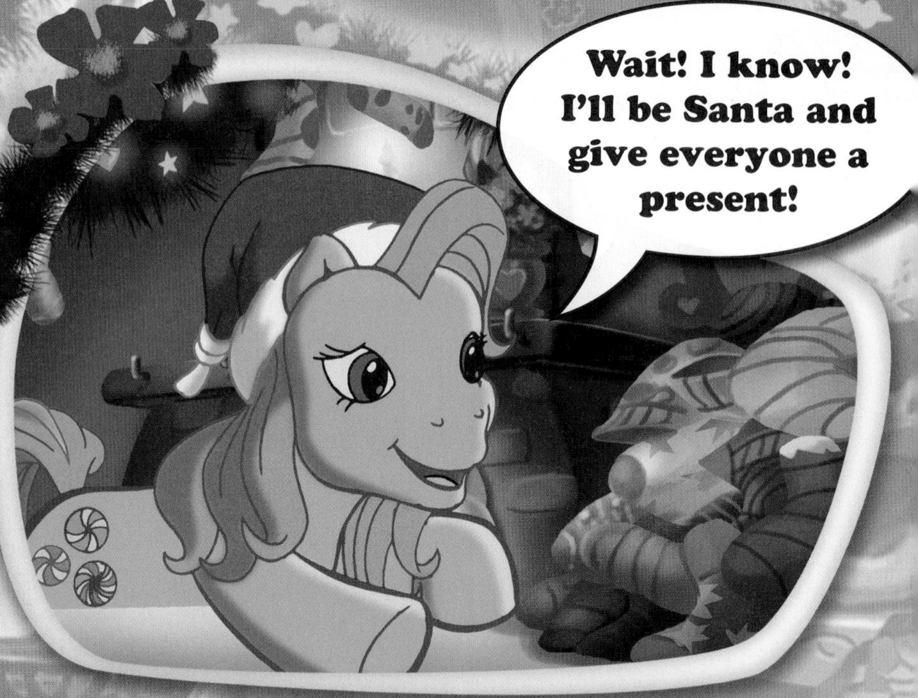
Wait! I know! I'll be Santa and give everyone a present!

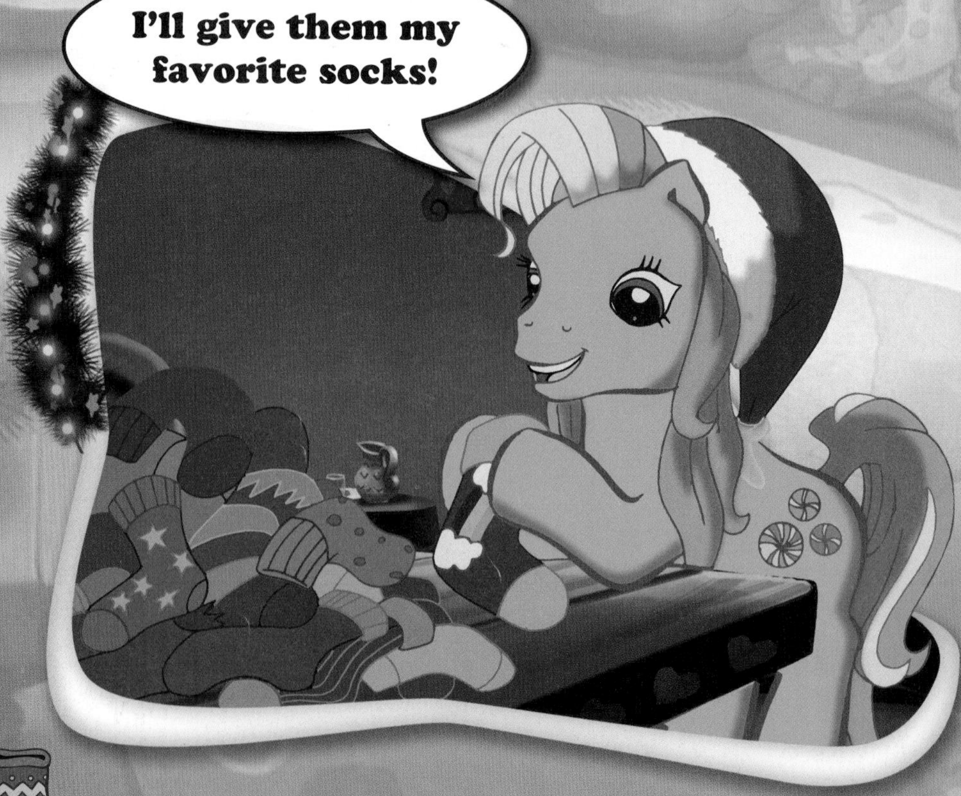
I'll give them my favorite socks!

At Pinkie Pie's house...

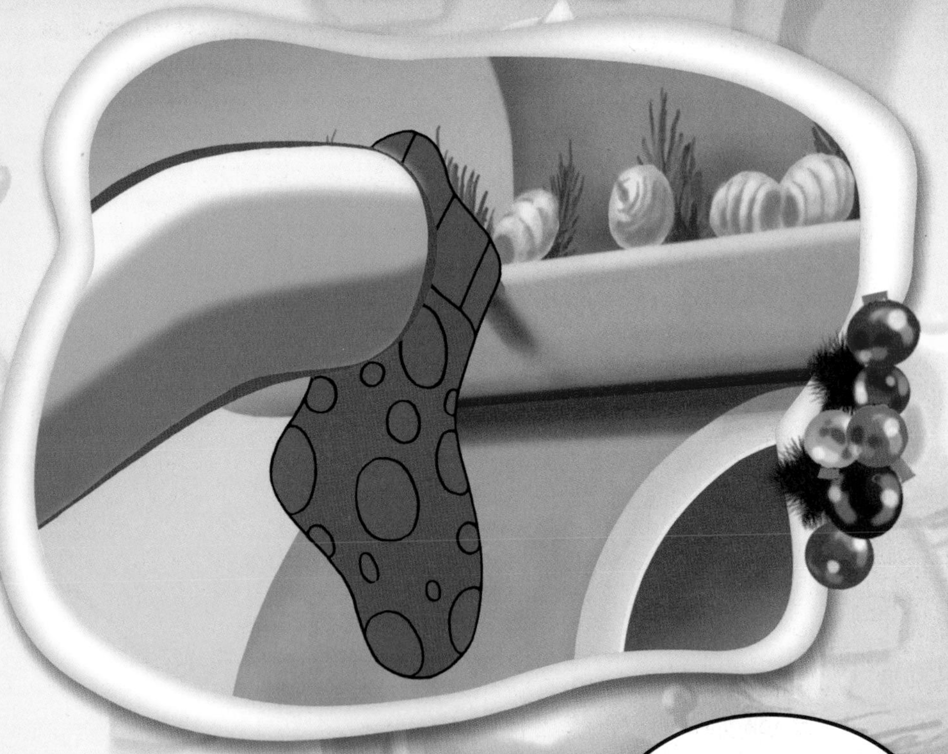

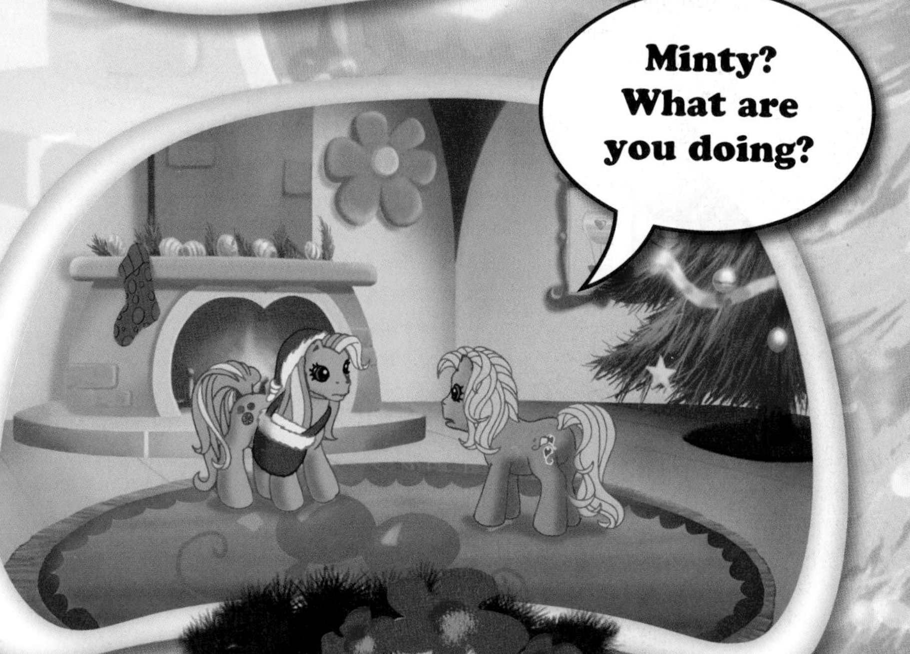
Minty? What are you doing?

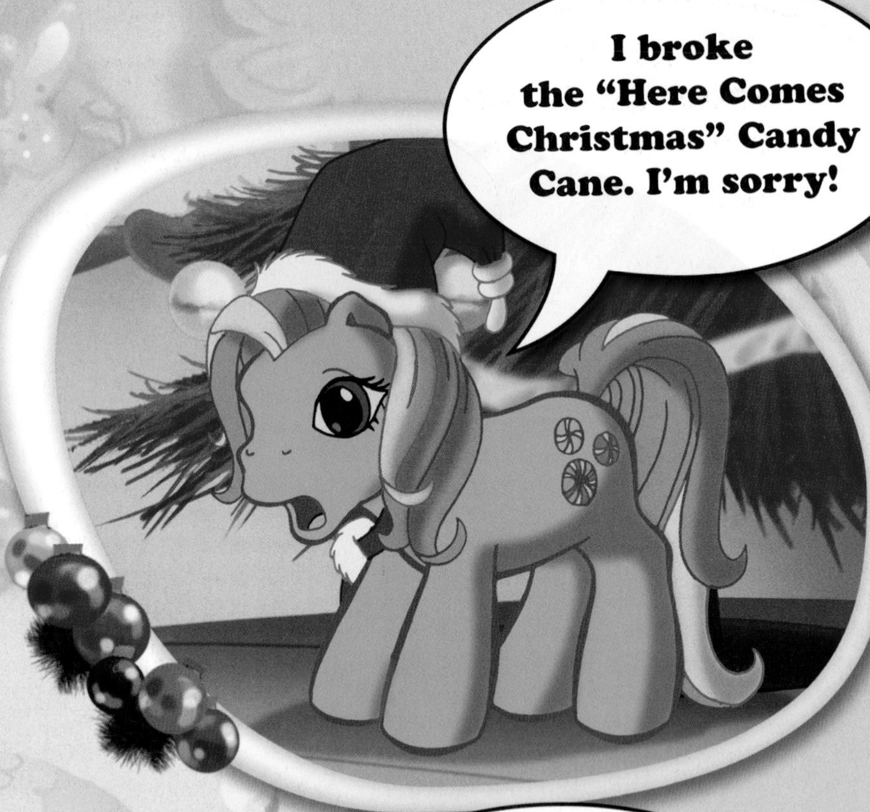
I broke the "Here Comes Christmas" Candy Cane. I'm sorry!

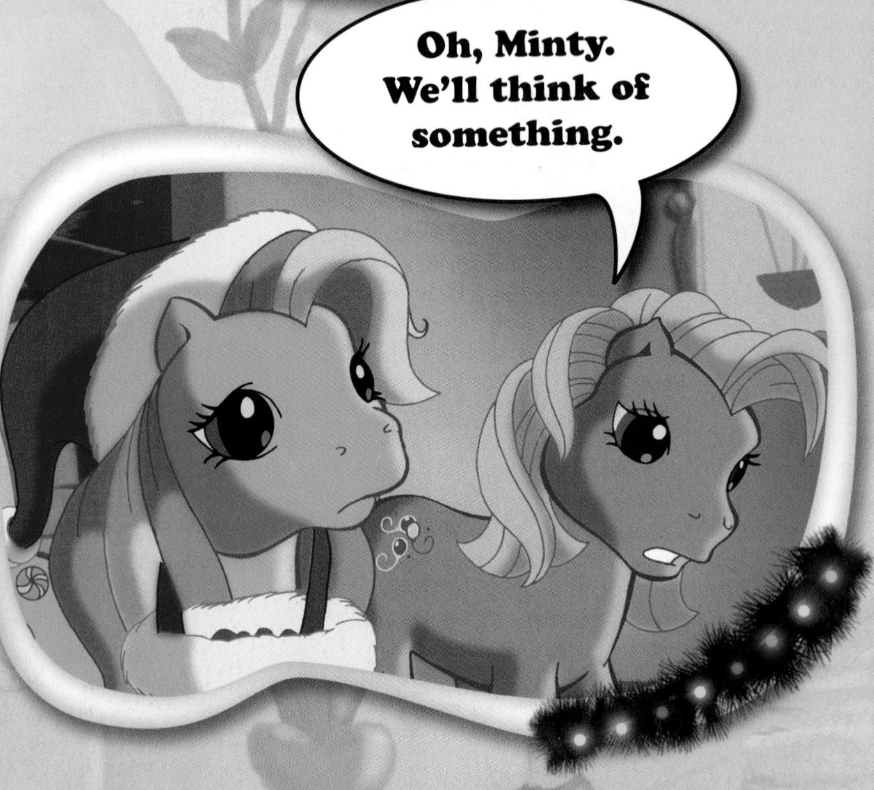
Oh, Minty. We'll think of something.

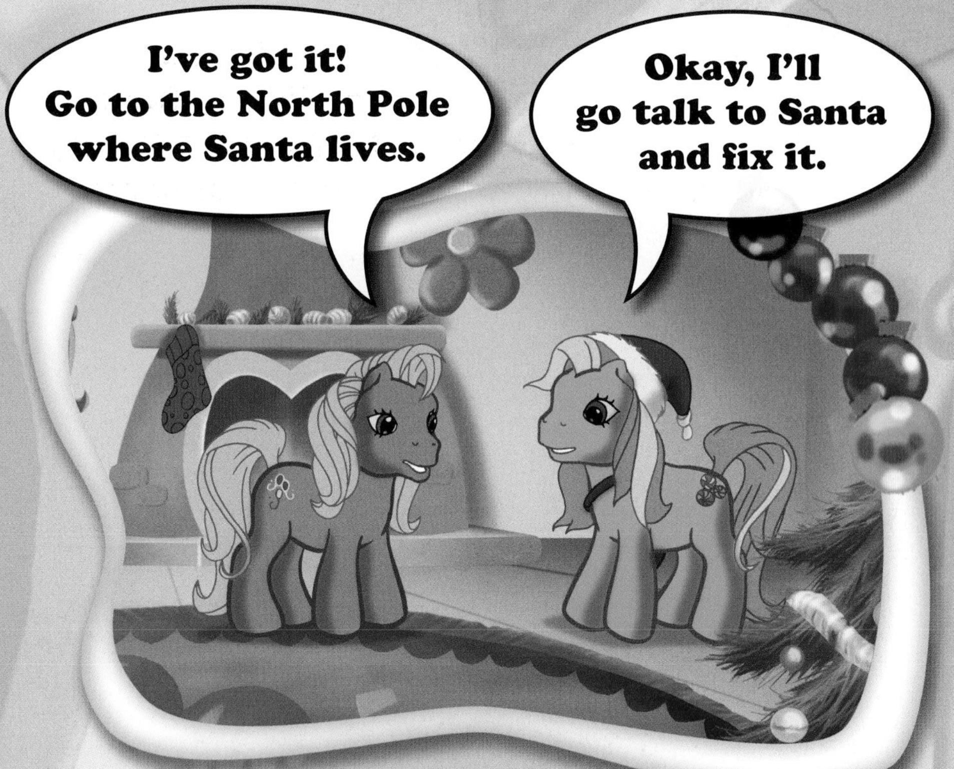
I've got it! Go to the North Pole where Santa lives.
Okay, I'll go talk to Santa and fix it.

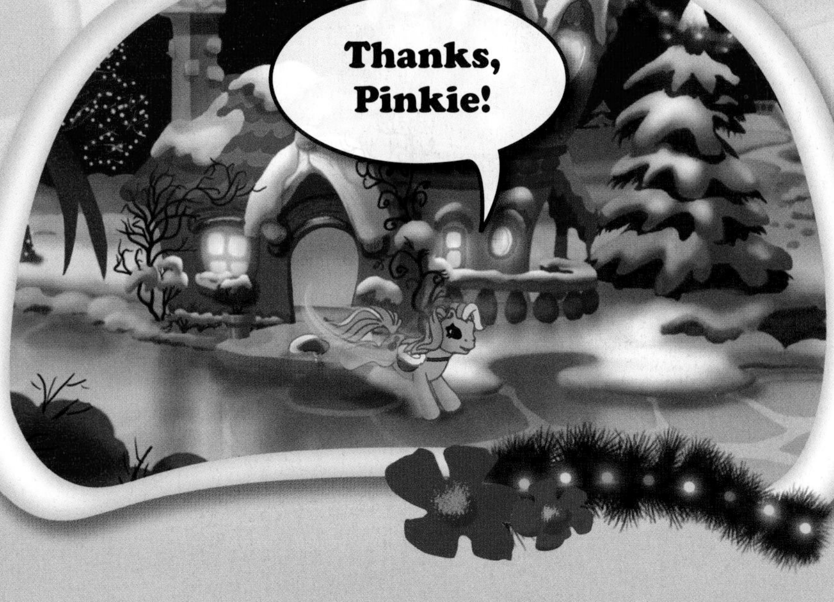
Thanks, Pinkie!

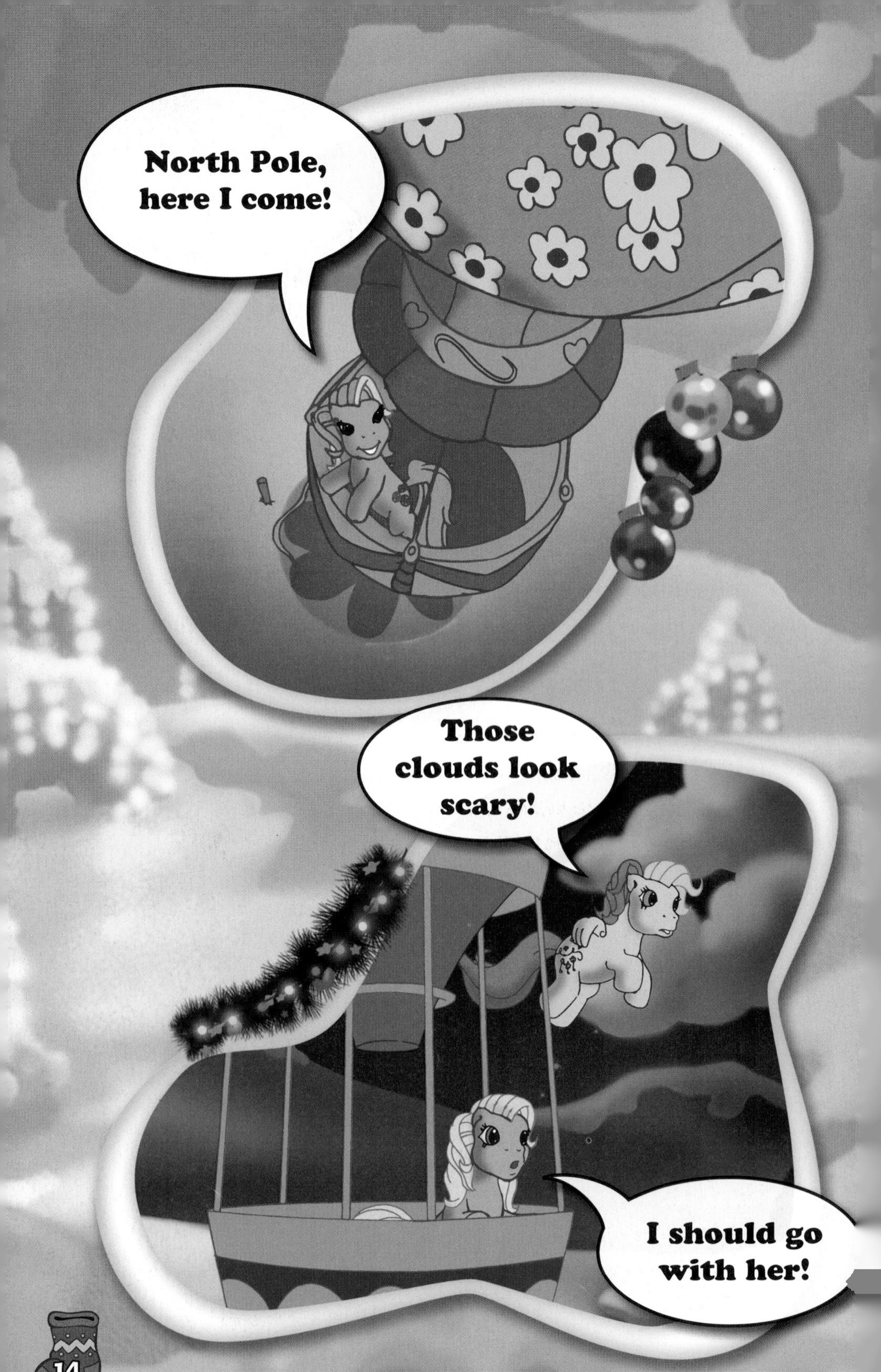
North Pole, here I come!
Those clouds look scary!
I should go with her!

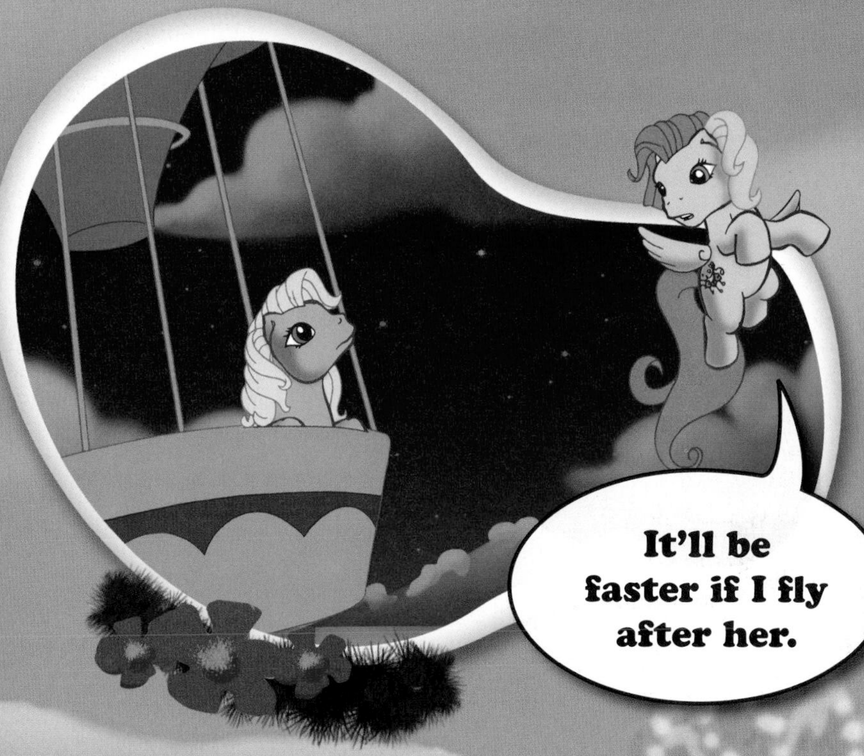
It'll be faster if I fly after her.

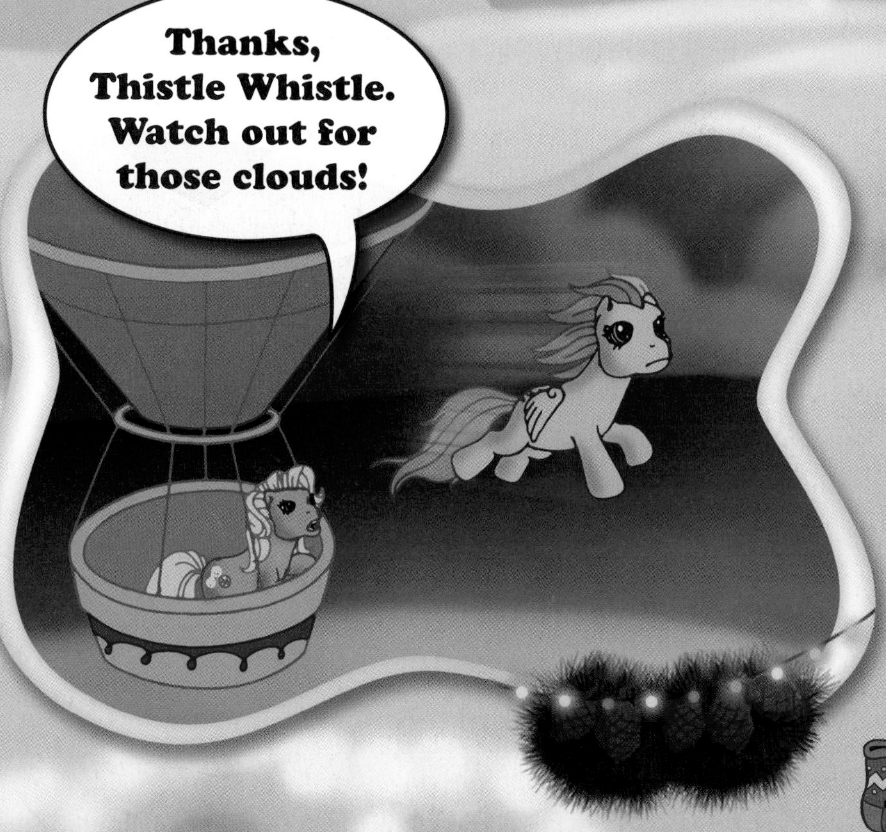
Thanks, Thistle Whistle. Watch out for those clouds!

At the Christmas tree...

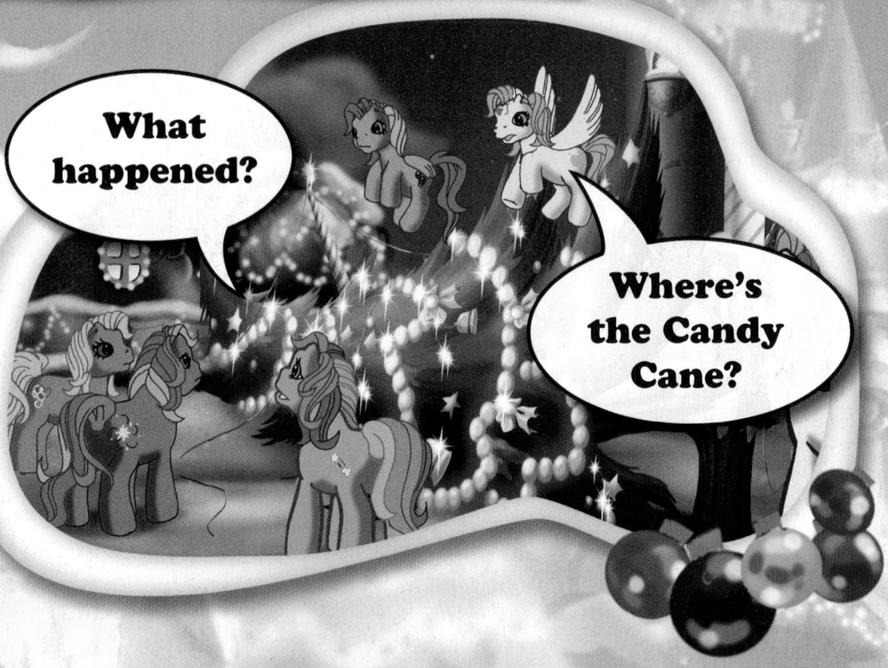
What happened?
Where's the Candy Cane?

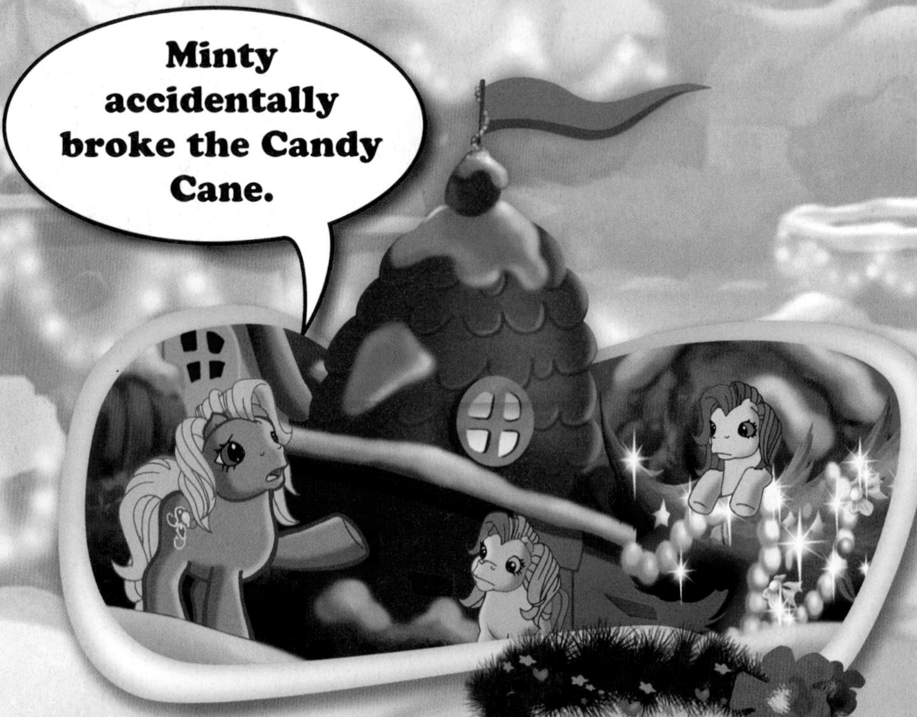
Minty accidentally broke the Candy Cane.

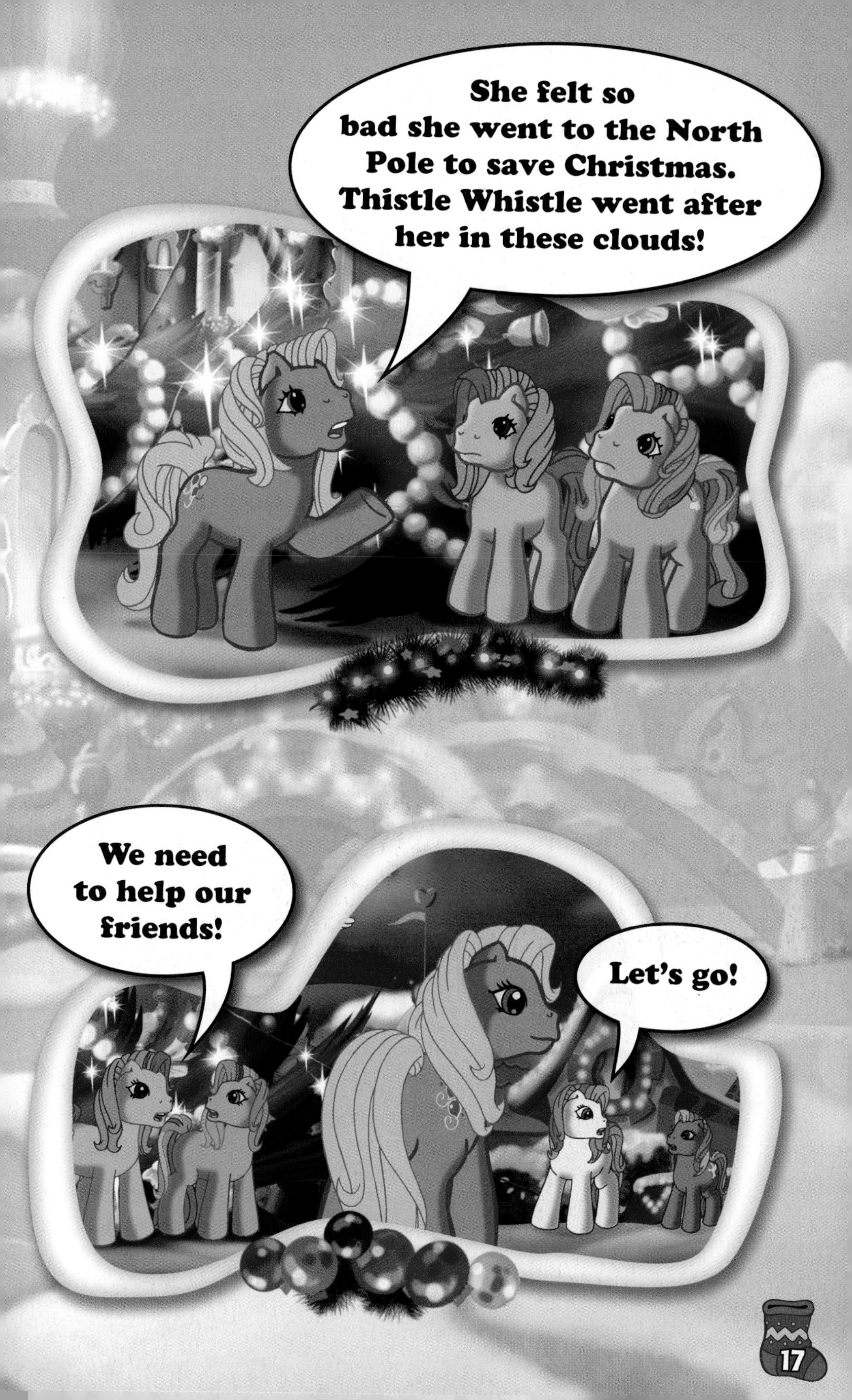
She felt so bad she went to the North Pole to save Christmas. Thistle Whistle went after her in these clouds!
We need to help our friends!
Let's go!

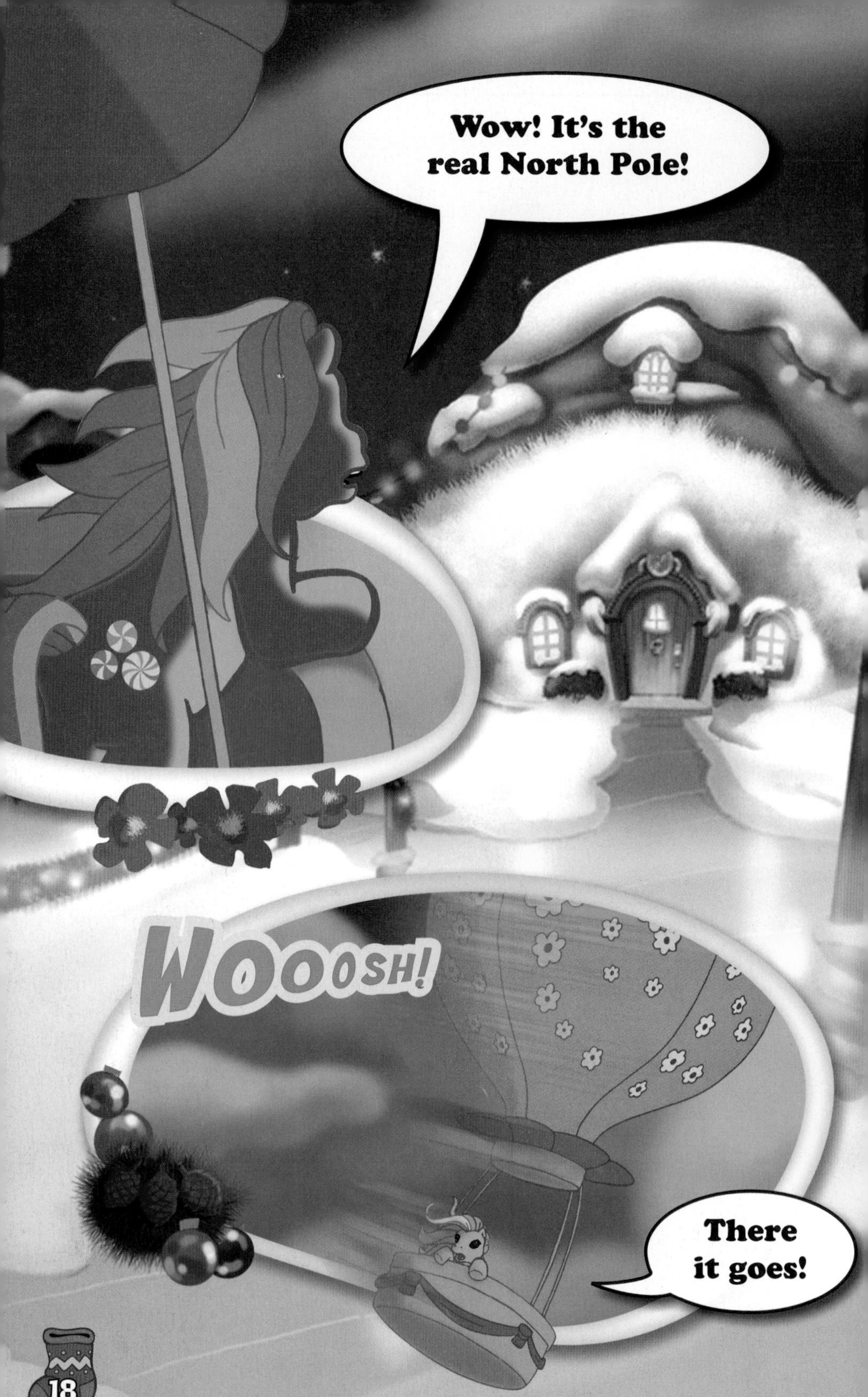
Wow! It's the real North Pole!
WOOOSH!
There it goes!

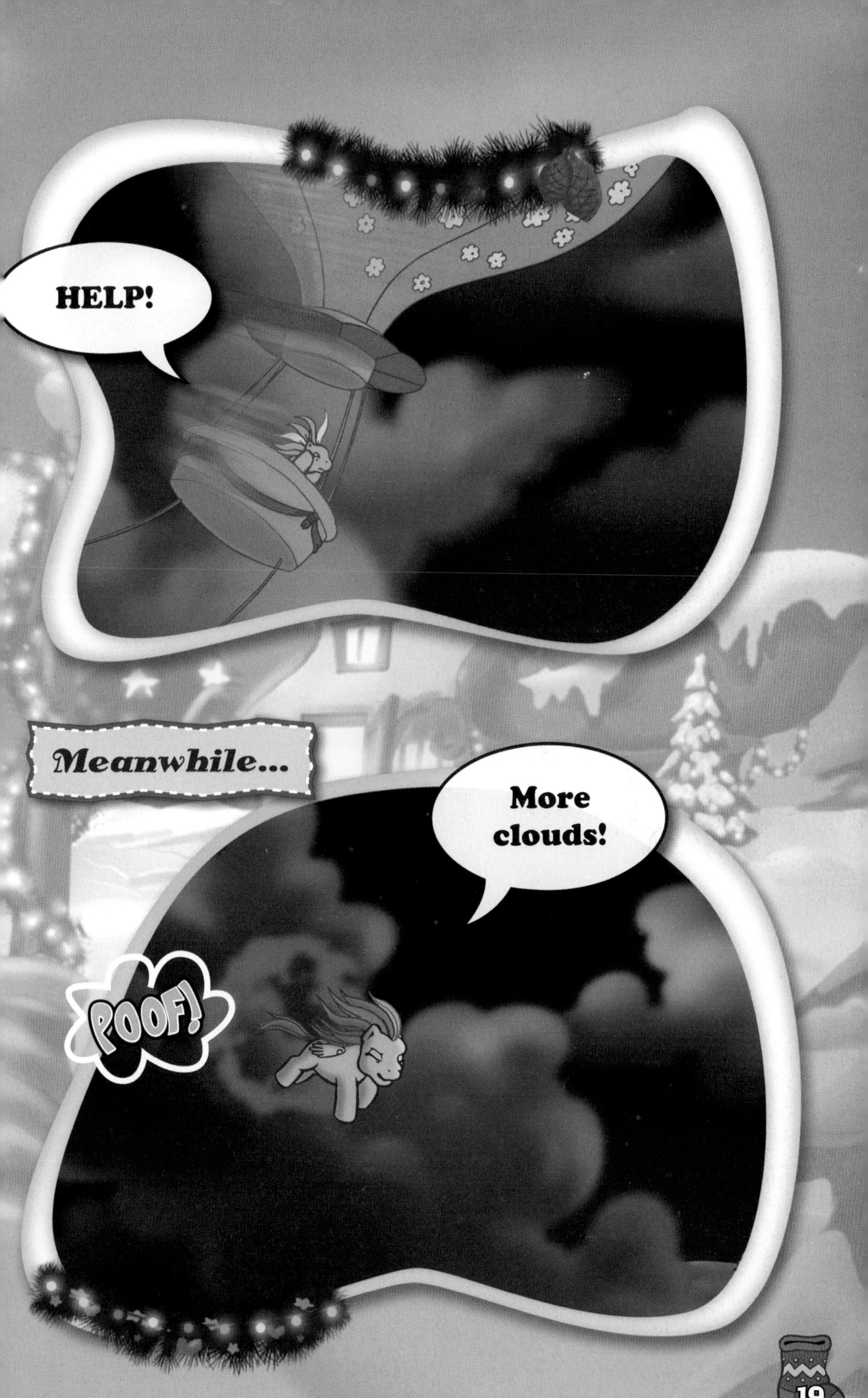
HELP!
Meanwhile...
More clouds!
POOF!

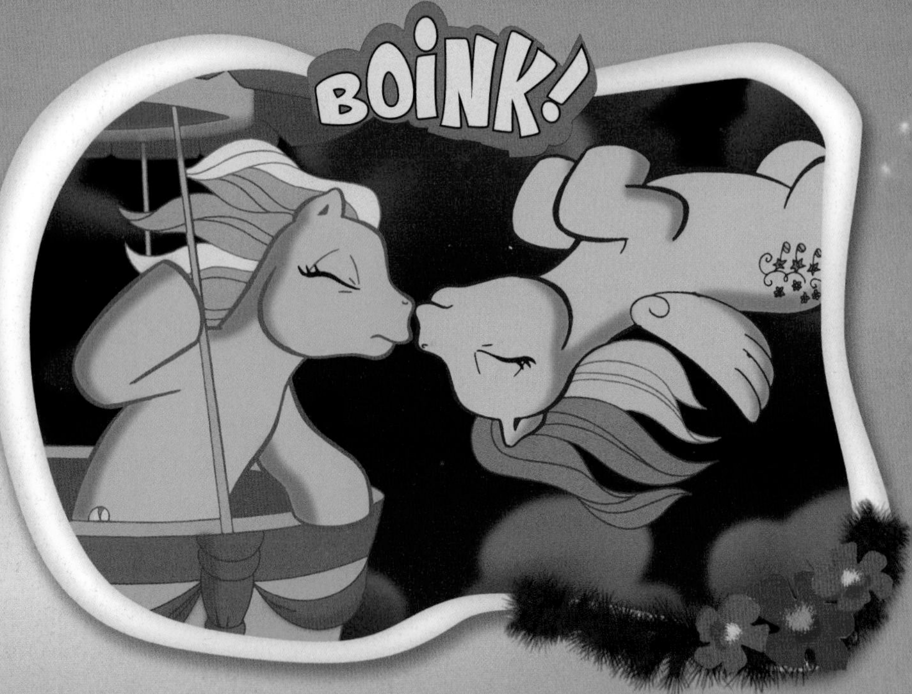
BOINK!

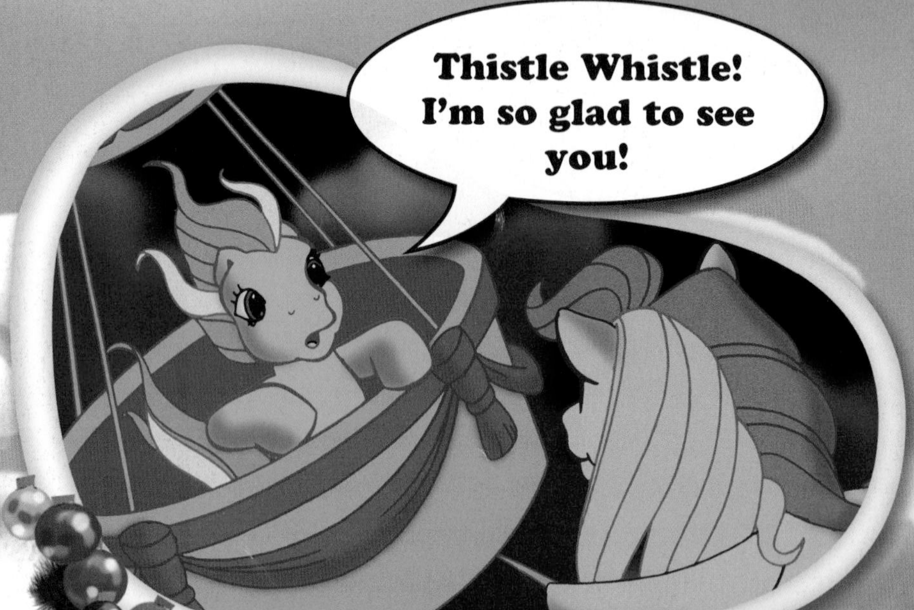
Thistle Whistle! I'm so glad to see you!

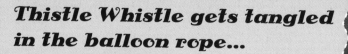

Thistle Whistle gets tangled in the balloon rope...

Oh no!

Look out!

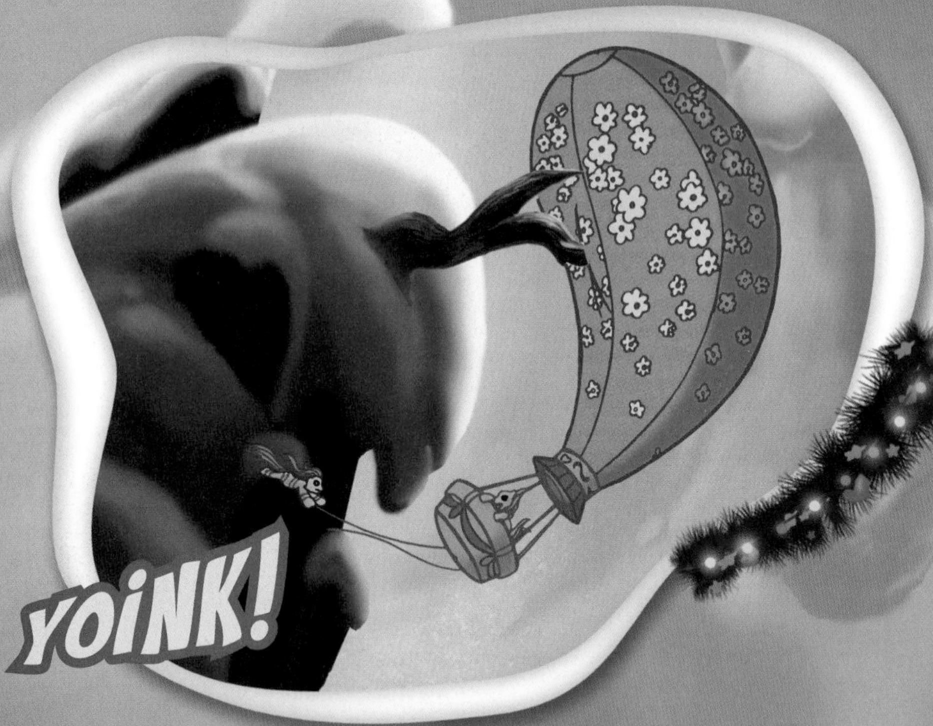
YOiNK!

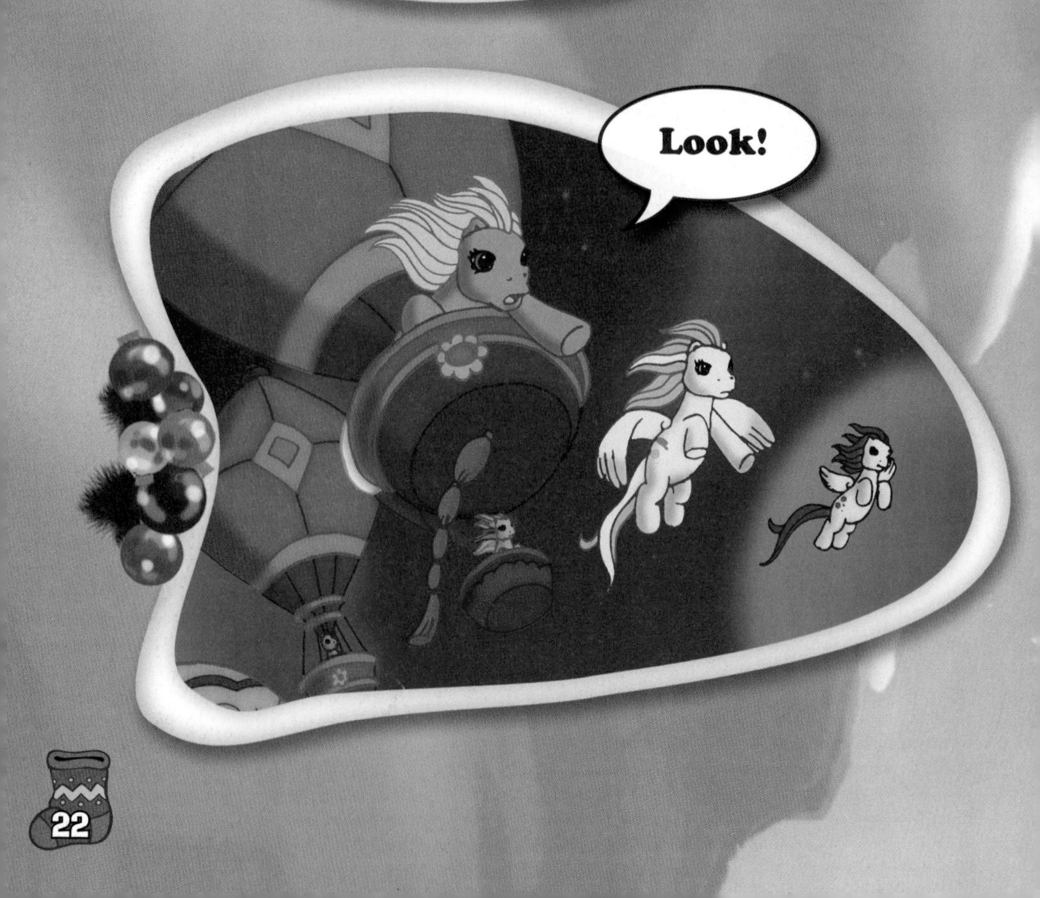
Look!

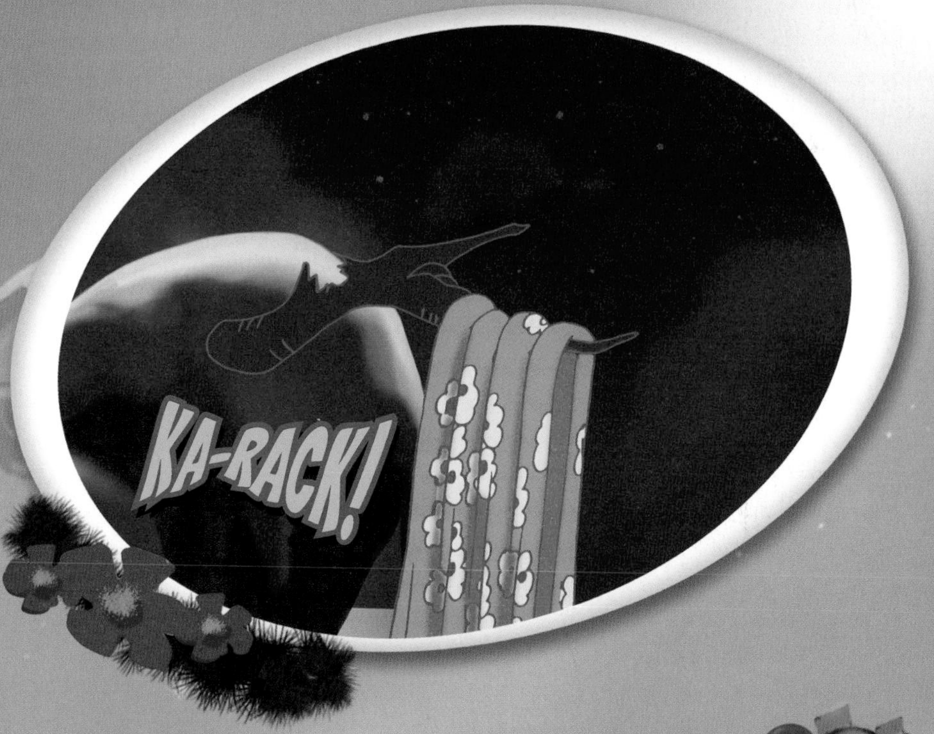
KA-RACK!
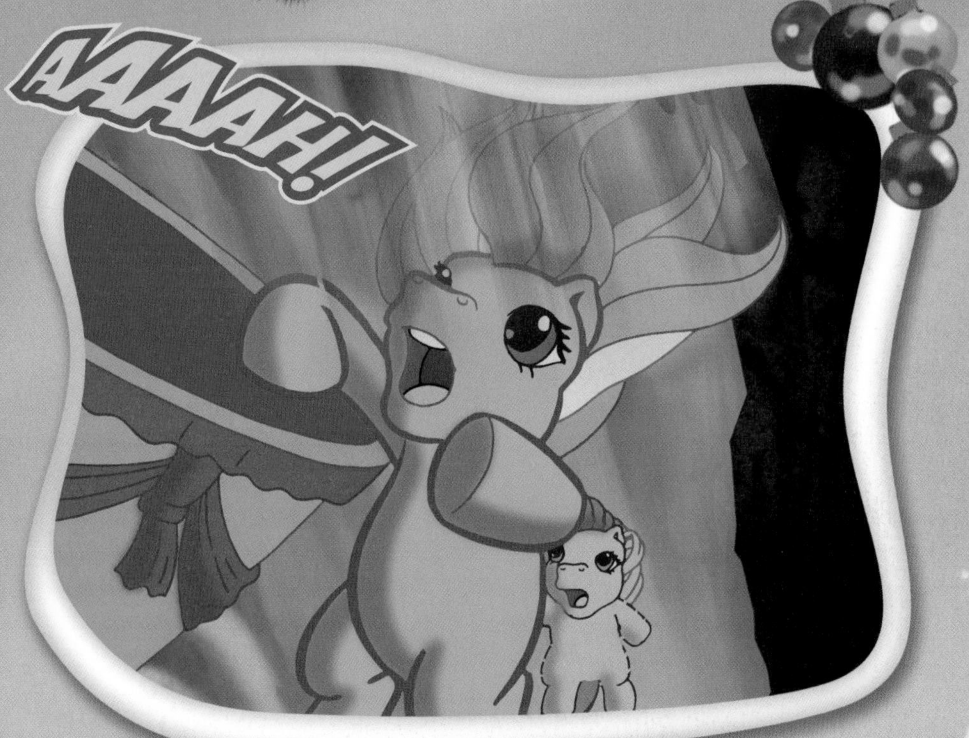
AAAAH!!

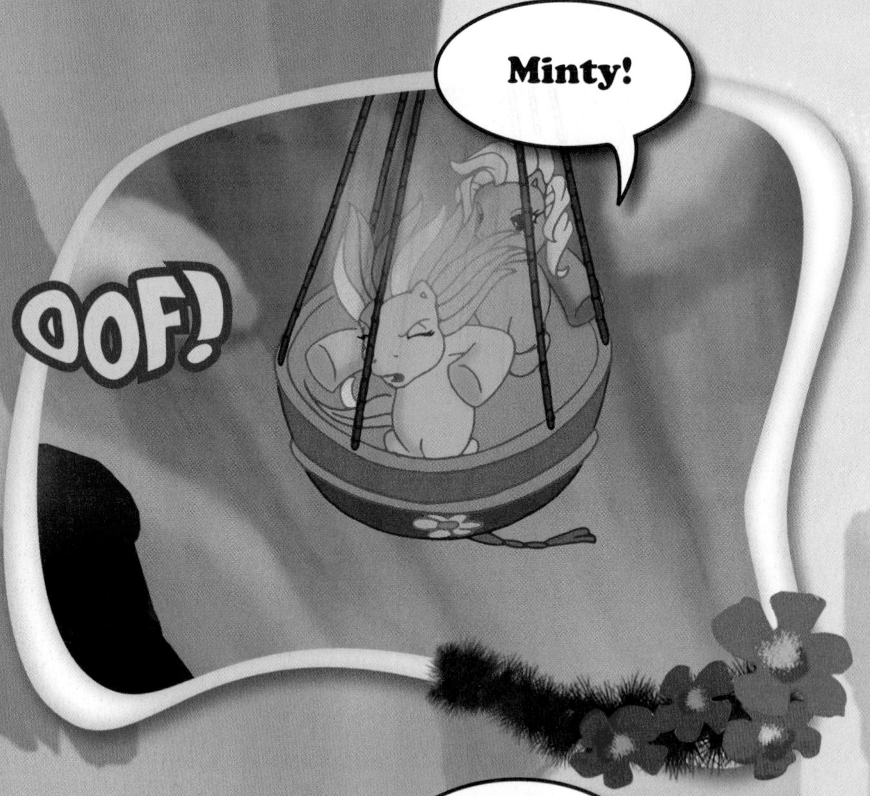
OOF!
Minty!

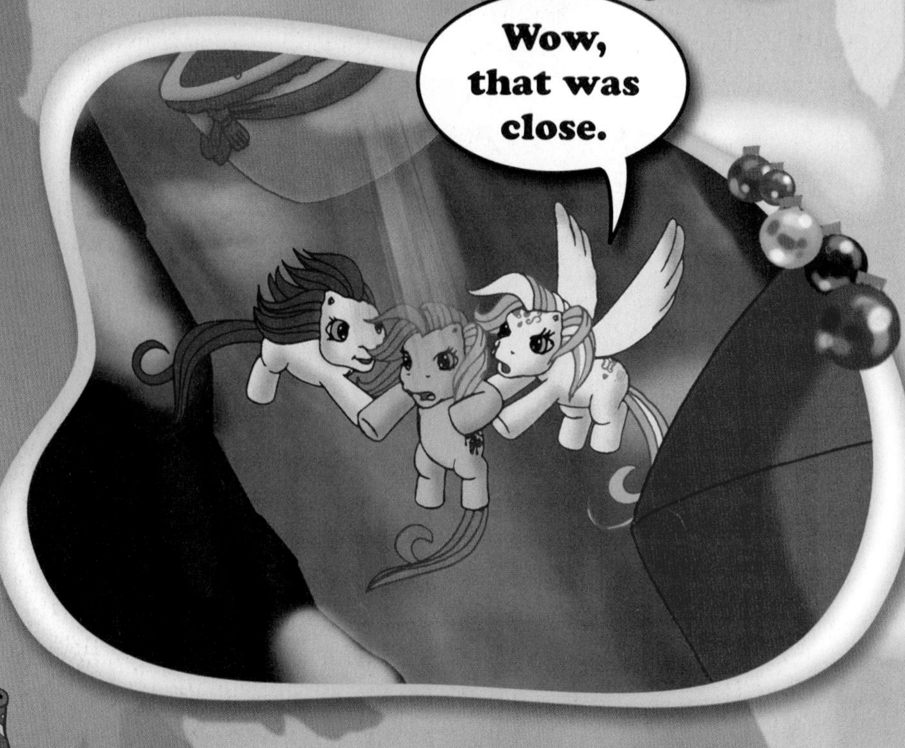
Wow, that was close.

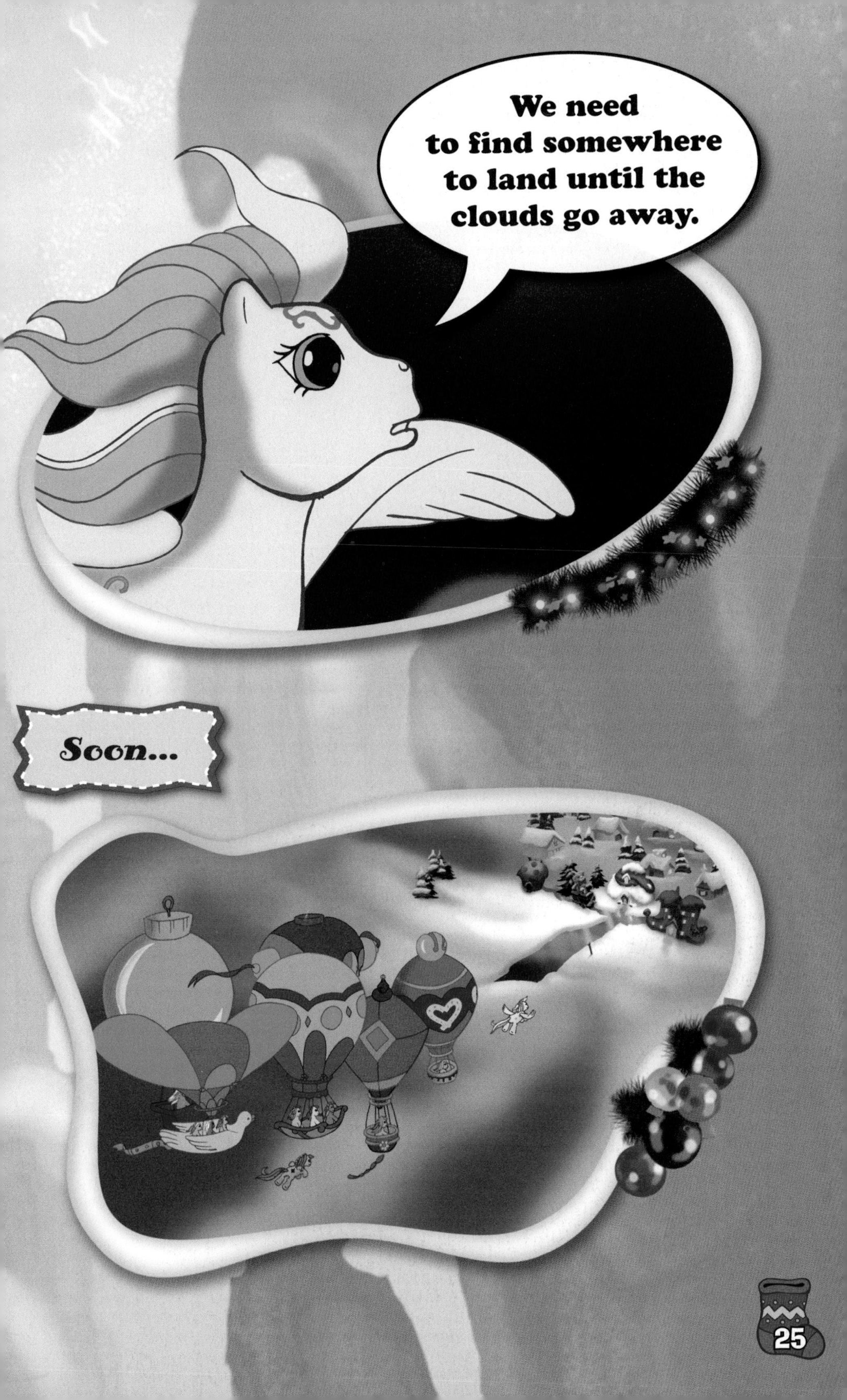
We need to find somewhere to land until the clouds go away.
Soon...

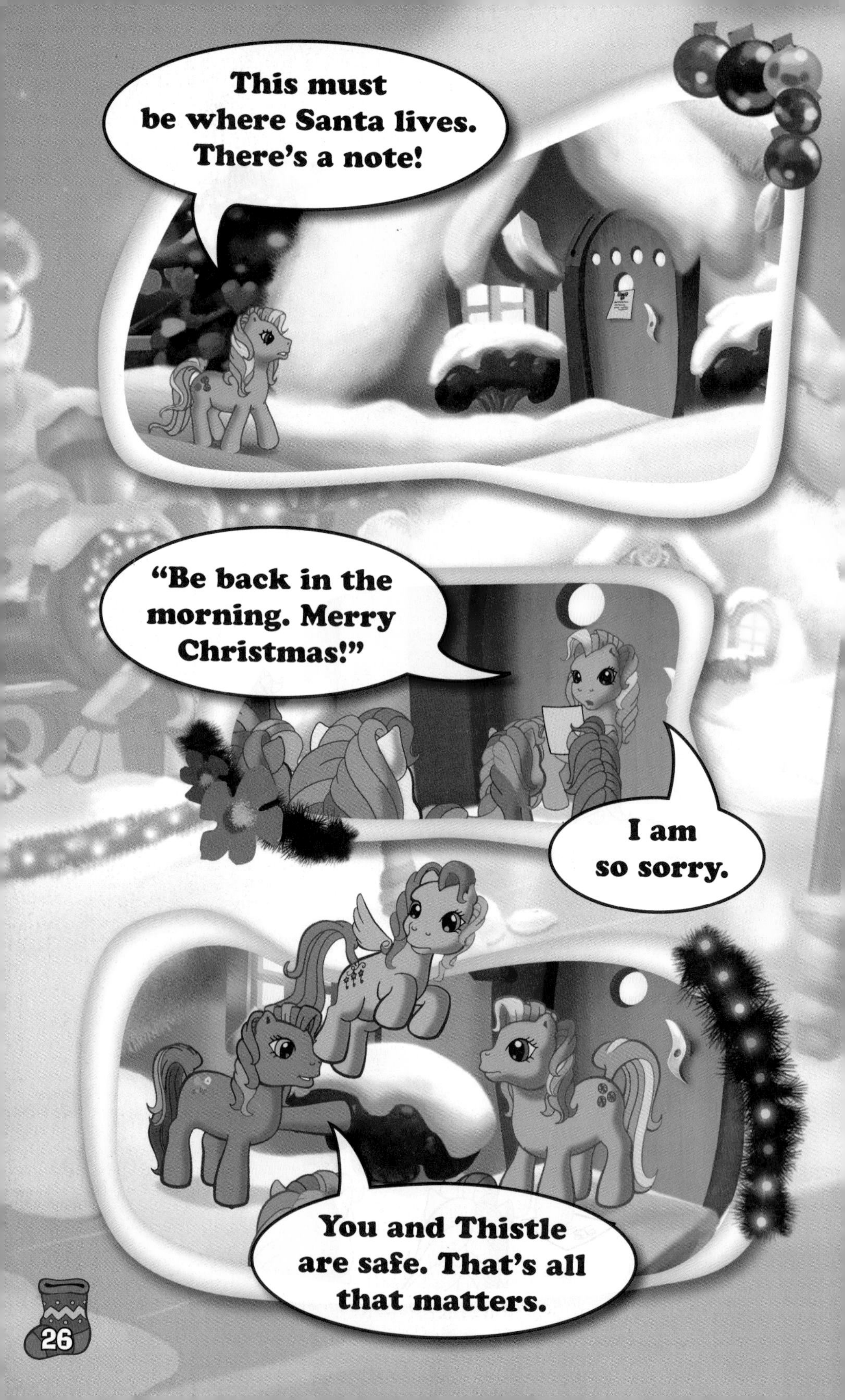
This must be where Santa lives. There's a note!
"Be back in the morning. Merry Christmas!"
I am so sorry.
You and Thistle are safe. That's all that matters.

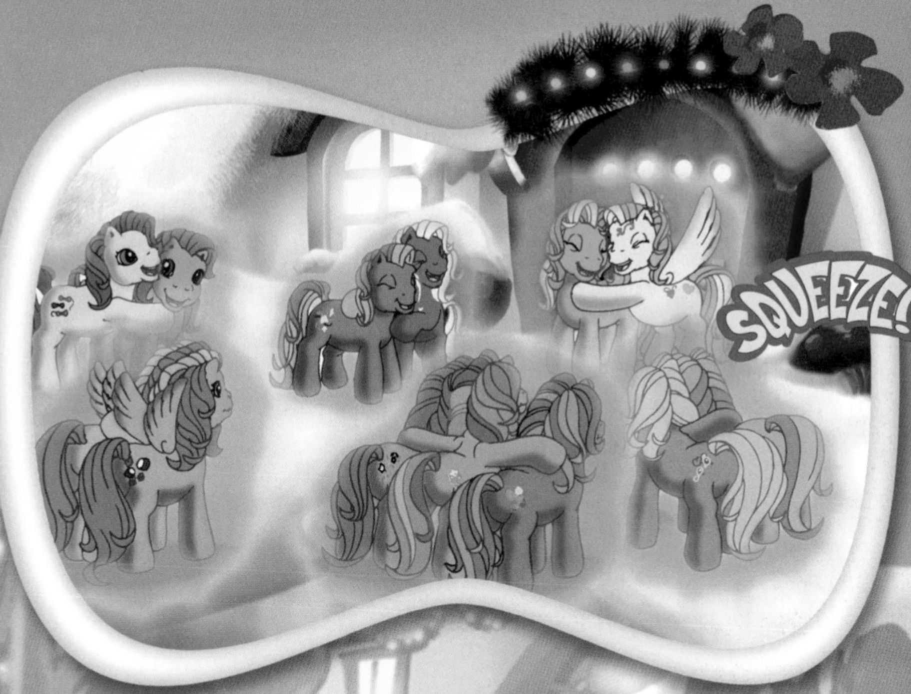
SQUEEZE!

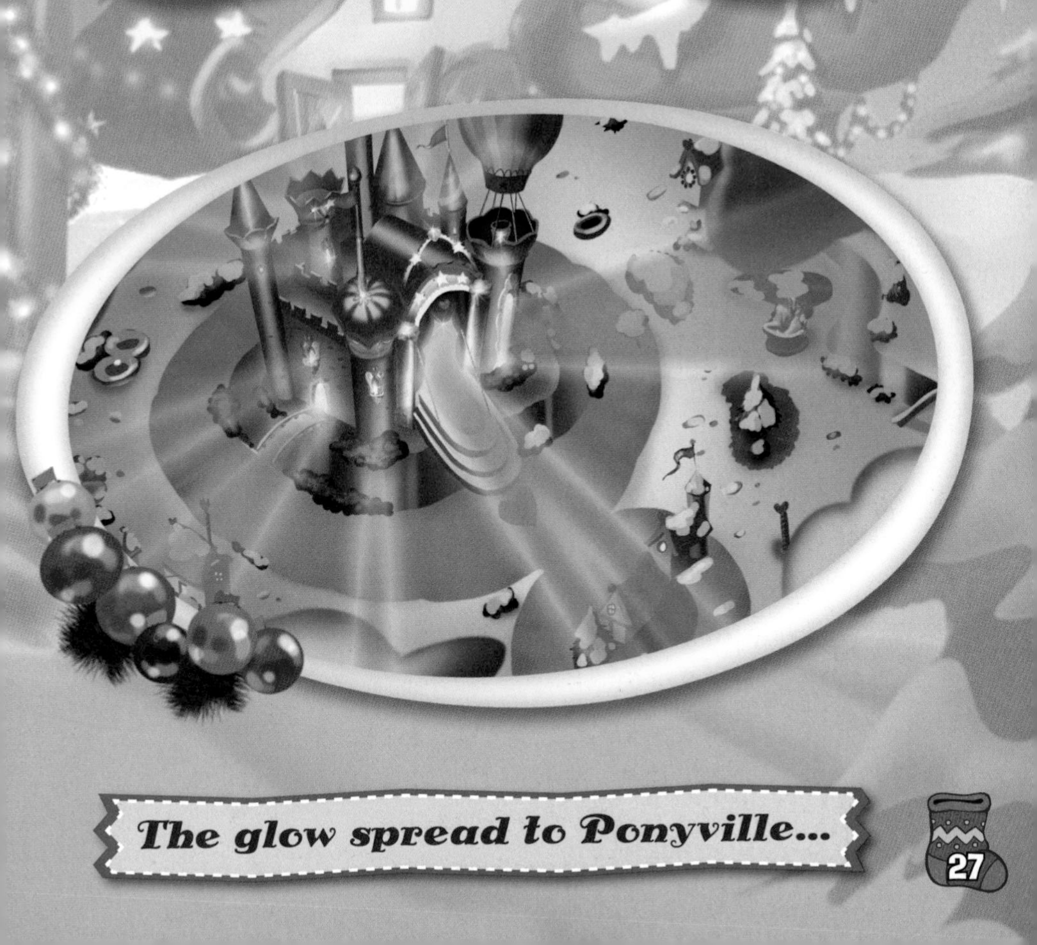

The glow spread to Ponyville...

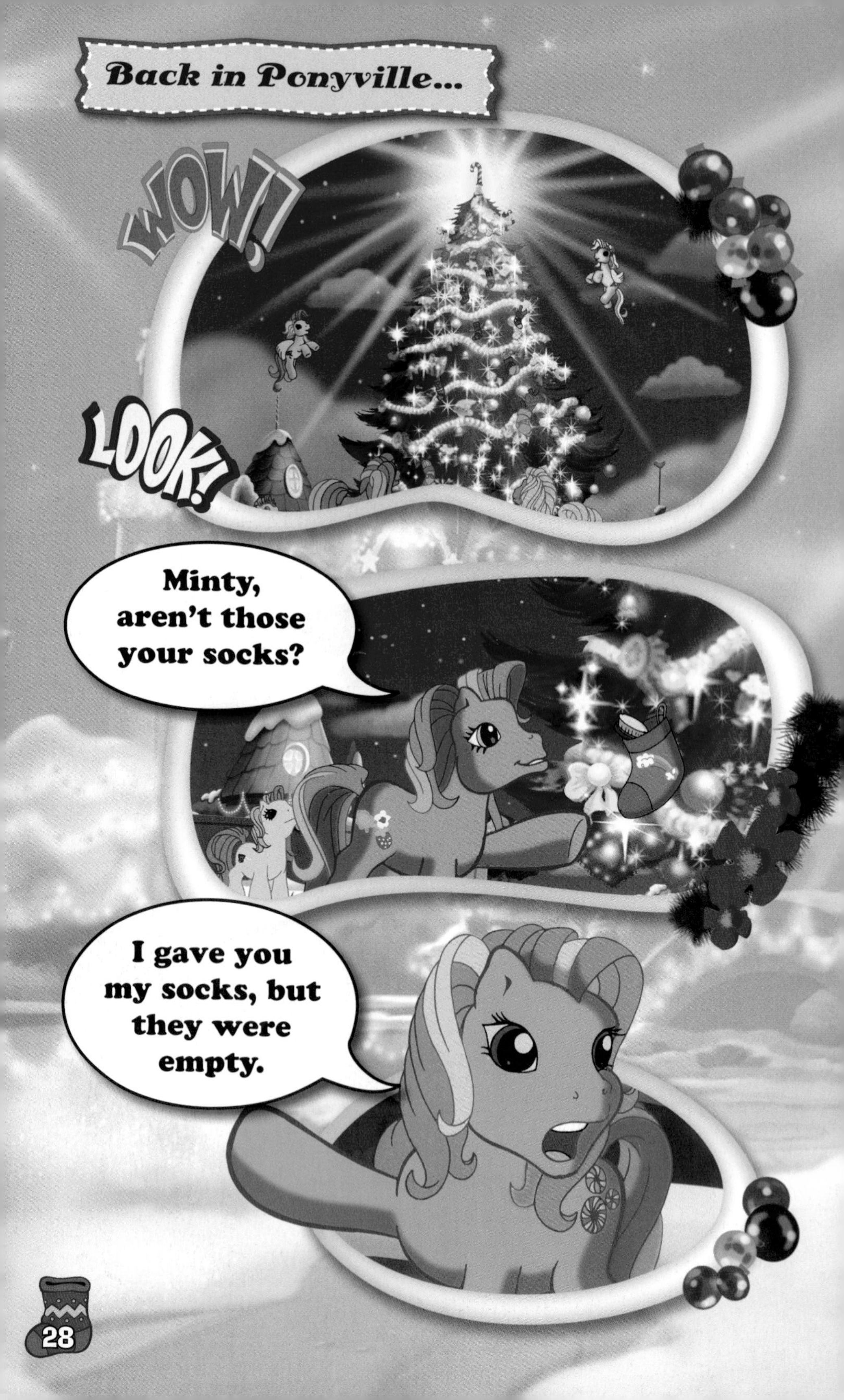
Back in Ponyville...
WOW!
LOOK!
Minty, aren't those your socks?
I gave you my socks, but they were empty.

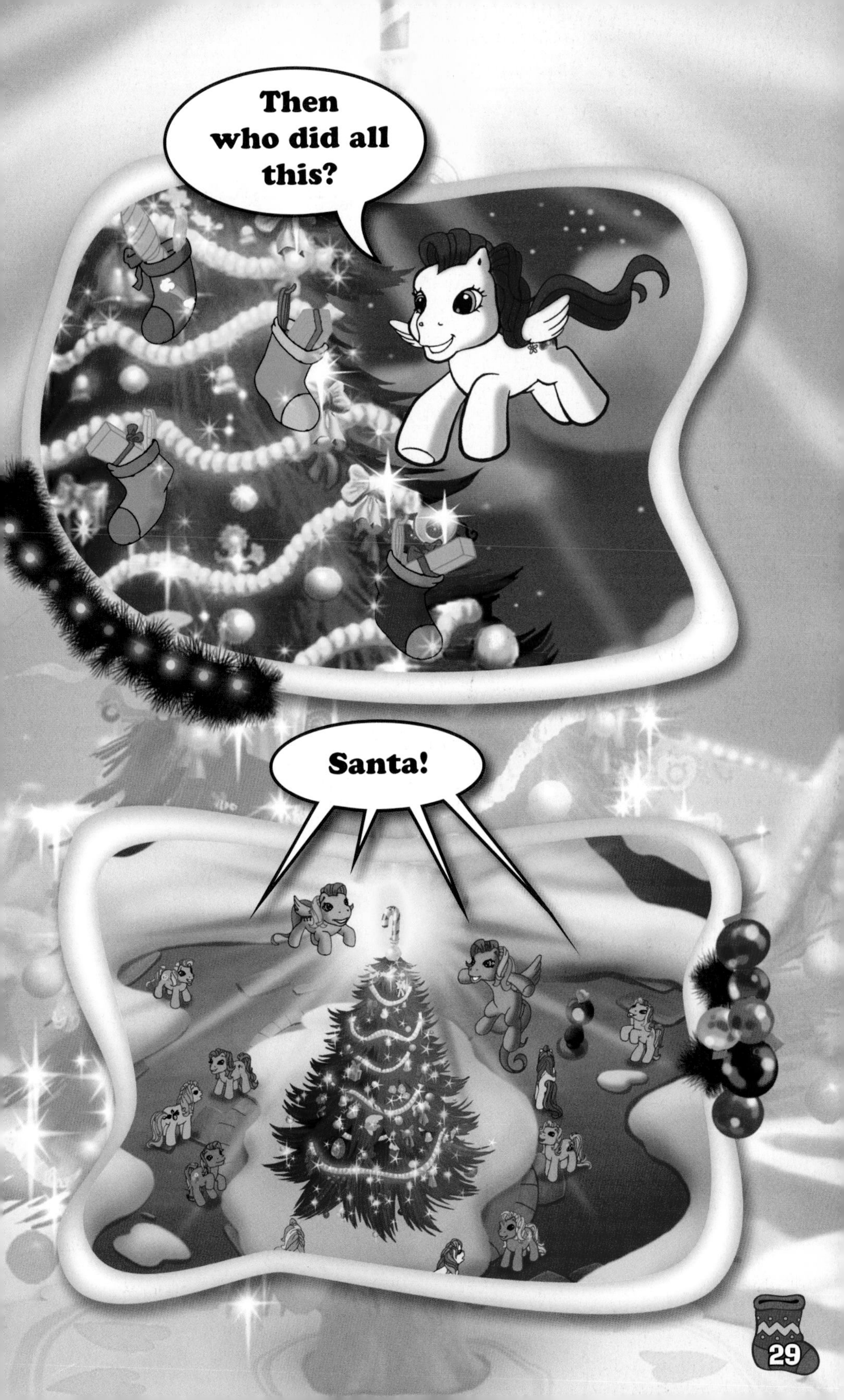
Then who did all this?
Santa!

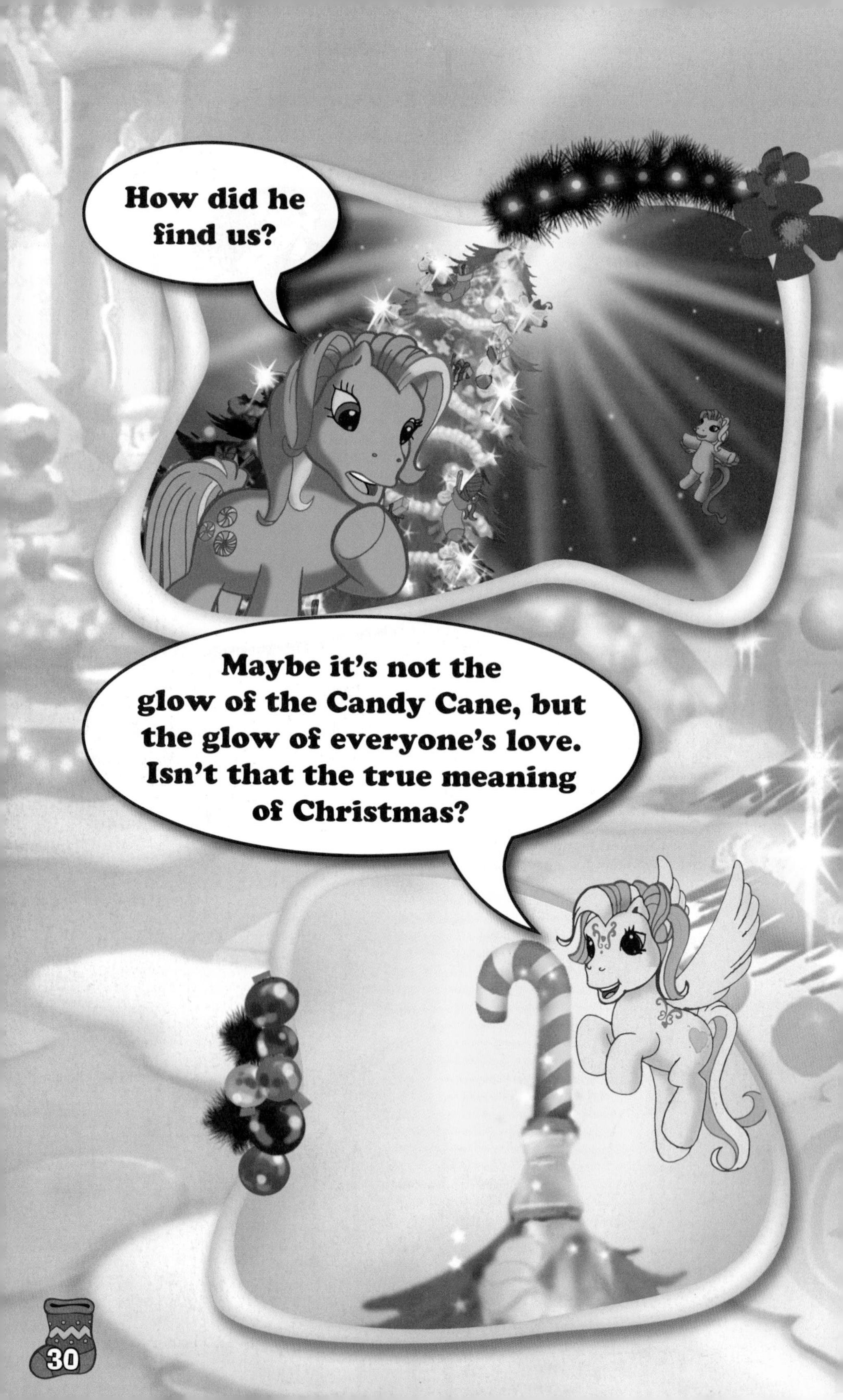
How did he find us?
Maybe it's not the glow of the Candy Cane, but the glow of everyone's love. Isn't that the true meaning of Christmas?

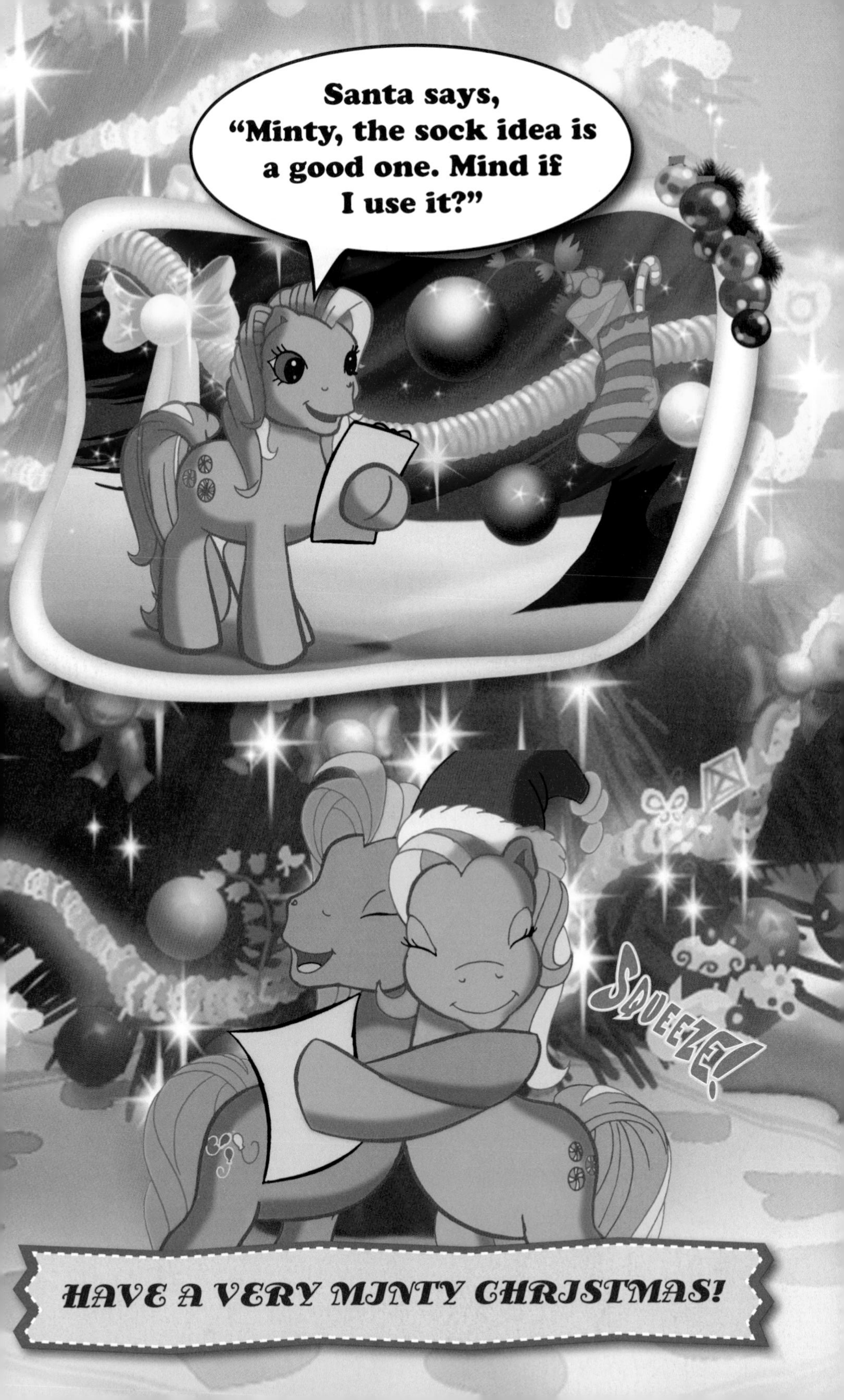
Santa says, "Minty, the sock idea is a good one. Mind if I use it?"
SQUEEZE!
HAVE A VERY MINTY CHRISTMAS!

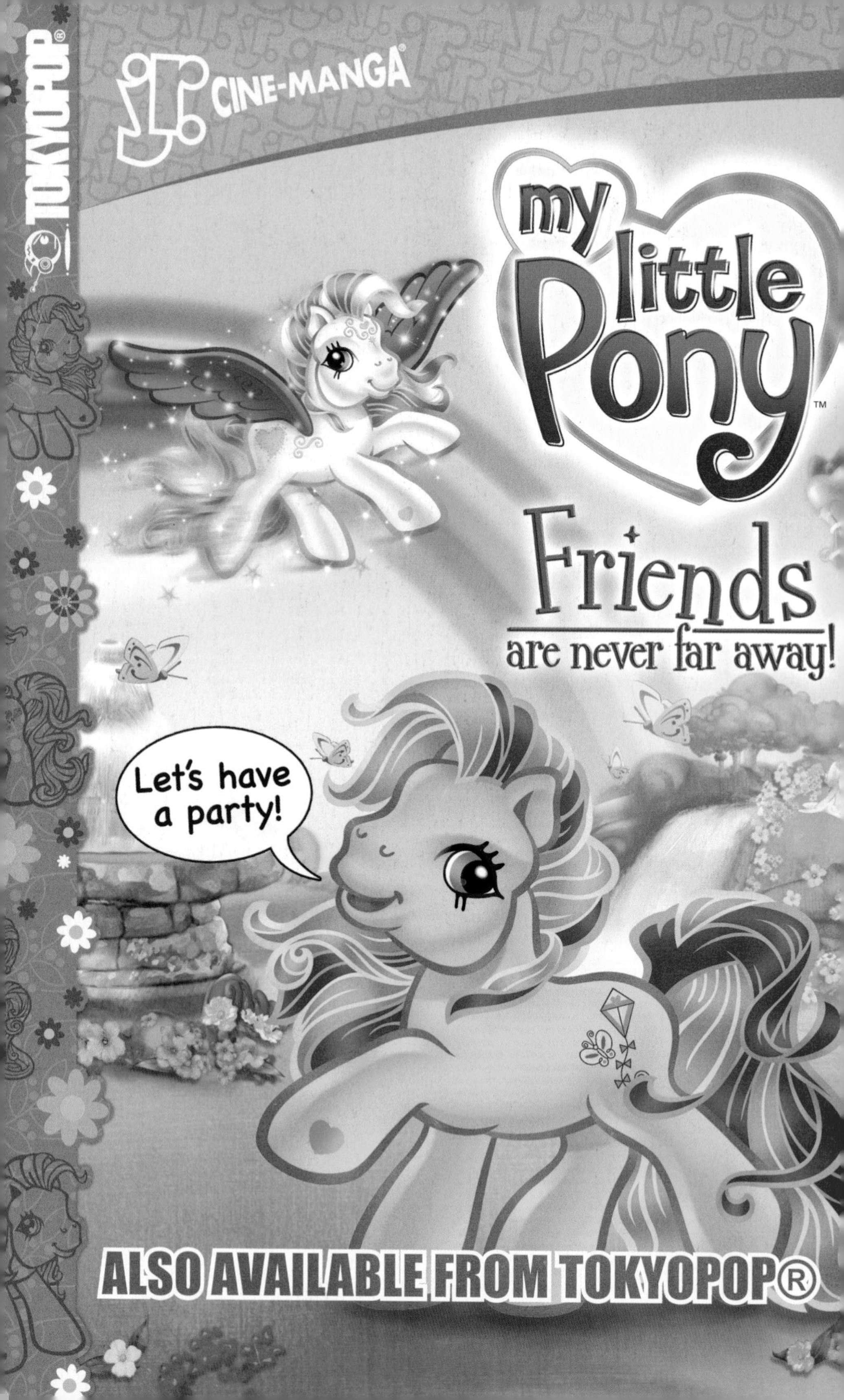
TOKYOPOP®
CINE-MANGA®
my little Pony™
Friends are never far away!
Let's have a party!
ALSO AVAILABLE FROM TOKYOPOP®